A Legal
Road M
for C

Ju

OASIS PRESS

The Oasis Press® / PSI Rese
Grants Pass, Oregon

D1501798

Published by The Oasis Press®

This publication is designed to provide accurate and authoritative information
in regard to the subject matter covered. It is sold with the understanding that the
publisher is not engaged in rendering legal, accounting, or other professional
service. If legal advice or other expert assistance is required, the services of a
competent professional person should be sought.
> — *from a declaration of principles jointly adopted by a committee of
> the American Bar Association and a committee of publishers.*

Editor: Janelle Davidson
Book Designer: Constance C. Dickinson
Compositor: Jan Olsson
Cover Designer: Steven Burns

Please direct any comments, questions, or suggestions regarding this book to
The Oasis Press®/PSI Research:

> Editorial Department
> P.O. Box 3727
> Central Point, OR 97502
> (541) 479-9464
> info@psi-research.com *email*

The Oasis Press® is a Registered Trademark of Publishing Services, Inc.,
an Oregon corporation doing business as PSI Research.

Library of Congress Cataloging-in-Publication Data

Gedge, Judy.
   A legal road map for consultants / Judy Gedge. — 1st ed.
      p.   cm. — (PSI successful business library)
   Includes index.
   ISBN 1-55571-460-9 (pbk.)
   1. Business consultants—Legal status, laws, etc.—United States.
I. Title. II. Series.
KF390.C65G43 1998
658.1'14—DC21
                         98-24138

Printed in the United States of America
First edition 10 9 8 7 6 5 4 3 2 1 0

 Printed on recycled paper when available.

To Mike and Sam with heaps of love.

Contents

Foreword

Congratulations for selecting this unusual book.

It's unusual in one respect because it is written by a lawyer in plain English, which means it's user friendly. But that's just one of several reasons why *A Legal Road Map for Consultants* should be on the bookshelf of every consultant.

First, this is the only book I'm aware of that deals exclusively with the legal issues of the consulting field. Second, it's a fast read. And third, it's an in-the-trenches field book —- not a scholarly work — filled with easy-to-apply information.

You'll quickly recognize that Judy Gedge understands the importance of establishing your consulting practice on a firm, legal footing, which can help you collect every dollar earned and then keep those earnings by protecting your personal assets. But she also understands that by helping to take the guesswork out of the legal side of consulting, your life can be less stressful.

In these pages, Judy helps to make you aware of major risks and how you can avoid unpleasant (and often costly) surprises that may occur if your consulting practice doesn't have the proper legal safeguards. While Judy is quick to refer you to your own attorney, this book can help to educate you on the foundational issues. Then, any private consultations with your lawyer can be more productive.

Long before you get to the last page, you'll sense that you've found a new friend who is concerned about your success. And indeed you have.

LEW WILLIAMS, publisher
Consulting Opportunities Journal

Preface

This book grew out of my practice as an honest-to-goodness small business attorney. Over the years, I have had the pleasure of representing hundreds of small business clients. In addition, I have presented legal workshops and seminars to small business owners and budding entrepreneurs for organizations such as the Small Business Administration and SCORE.

Over the last few years, I noticed a tremendous increase in the number of people starting their own consulting practices. Whether they call themselves consultants or free-lancers or even self-employed professionals, there's one thing they all have in common. They each have a particular field of expertise which they recognized was of value in the marketplace. You may be in a similar position. If you're thinking of starting your own consulting practice or are already in business for yourself, congratulations! Congratulations on capitalizing on your expertise and allowing yourself the freedom to be your own boss.

In my experience as an attorney advising consultants about the legal aspects of their business, the same questions come up. What kind of potential liability will I face in my consulting practice? Should I form a limited liability company? How about a Delaware corporation? I'm just a little guy, why do I need liability insurance? Isn't a handshake as good as a written agreement? These are just a few of the questions that consultants frequently ask me. If you have questions like these or are just plain confused, let me help to de-mystify the legal aspects of your consulting business.

I have tried to make this book user-friendly by using plain English and plenty of real-life examples. It's not an academic tome and it's not a legal encyclopedia. It's meant to help you see your way through the thicket of legal questions often faced by consultants. Since I can't sit down with each one of you individually to answer your legal questions, I've tried to do the next best thing by writing down the explanations and advice that I give to my own clients. I hope you will find it helpful.

So make yourself comfortable. Grab a cup of coffee or a tall glass of iced tea and come with me. I'll explain in easy-to-understand language what you need to know to properly structure and run your consulting business.

Acknowledgments

The author gratefully acknowledges the following people who have provided valuable help with the preparation of this book: Richard Reynolds, CPA, who kindly reviewed the tax aspects of the book; Attorney Guy Ortoleva who assisted with the intellectual property portions of the book; and Emmett Ramey and all the other folks at The Oasis Press who have been a pleasure to work with. In addition, the author sincerely acknowledges the enthusiastic support that she has received from her extended family of Alperts and Dambiers as well as her professional family, Attorney Mark J. Svonkin and Gloria Gora.

Chapter 1

Potential Liability
It's Lurking in Every Corner

Jim started his software consulting business three years ago and has never been happier. After working for a large corporation for 15 years, he really enjoys being his own boss. Because it seems the simplest way, Jim is operating his business as a sole proprietor. He has been hired by a new client for a large project and has brought his colleague, Bill, on board to help. En route to the client's office one morning, Bill accidentally hit a bicyclist who swerved into traffic on a busy road. And there Jim's troubles began.

The bicyclist is seriously injured and the next thing Jim knows, he and Bill are both being sued. Unfortunately, Bill forgot to pay his auto insurance premium, and the potential damages are way over a million dollars. Now Jim has an attachment on his house, is paying a lawyer to defend him, and is wondering "How could this have happened to me?"

Could Jim have done anything to protect himself from personal liability in this situation? The answer is a simple and resounding yes. If Jim had formed a corporation, or other entity of limited liability, he would not have exposed himself to personal liability for his colleague's actions. But as a sole proprietor, there is no legal distinction between Jim and his business. This means that all of Jim's assets are exposed to satisfy a judgment that arises out of his business operations. The most significant benefit of forming an entity like a corporation is that it provides you with protection from personal liability.

One of the first issues you will need to address in starting your consulting business is the type of business entity that will work best for you. A sole proprietorship may seem the simplest way, but don't forget to look closely at the hidden costs, the potential liability that you are exposing yourself to.

The options may at first seem overwhelming. You probably know something about corporations, S corporations, and C corporations. Maybe you've heard about the new limited liability company (LLC) and are wondering about it. In some states there's an even newer type of entity, a limited liability partnership (LLP). Perhaps you're thinking about operating as a sole proprietor, like Jim, or are considering a general partnership. If you are confused by all of these options, take heart. In this chapter you'll learn how to identify the areas of potential liability associated with your particular business. In the next chapter you'll learn about the variety of business entities and how to choose the right one for your business.

Every business has risks associated with it. If you were in the business of manufacturing chain saws, it would be easy to see that you run the risk of a customer being injured while using your product. The next thing you know you are being sued for damages on a claim that the chain saw was unreasonably dangerous or had a design defect. These are known as product liability lawsuits. You've probably read lots of newspaper stories about this kind of lawsuit. Remember the customer who got a huge verdict against McDonald's because her coffee was too hot?

As a consultant, the chain-saw type of liability is not likely to be of major concern to you. But just because you aren't selling chain saws doesn't mean that your business is risk free. Liability can arise, for instance, from your consulting services, under contracts, or even for the acts of others, your partners, your employees, and sometimes even your colleagues. You will want to look closely at the kinds of liability that you may be exposing yourself to in your consulting business.

Liability Arising from Your Consulting Services

Assume that you're a management information systems (MIS) computer consultant. You've worked for many years as an employee of a big insurance company. Now you've been offered early retirement and see a golden opportunity to cash out of the company and start a business of your own in MIS consulting.

In the old days you might have referred to this as job-shopping, but these days you'd be called a consultant. You have plenty of contacts in the industry and have already been approached by a few colleagues about providing consulting services for their companies. In fact, you may even be retained by your old company for consulting projects from time to time. The bottom line is that business prospects look great.

You will face potential liability as a result of the very services that you will be providing to your clients. Say, for instance, that you've been retained to develop and install a new software system for your old company. You complete the job and later receive a phone call telling you that not only is the system failing to perform but it's also interfering with other unrelated software programs, resulting in a total shutdown of the division's computer systems.

The next thing you know, you've received a demand letter from in-house counsel seeking payment of tens of thousands of dollars in damages alleging that you've provided faulty consulting services. The lawyer further recommends that you put your insurance carrier on notice of the claim against you.

"Hold on a minute," you say to yourself. "I'm doing exactly the same work that I used to do and for the same company, and they never threatened to sue me before. Sure, maybe I made a little mistake, but I can fix that, and anyway there's no need to make a federal case out of it."

You may be performing exactly the same services as a consultant that you did when you were an employee, but there's one major difference; as a consultant, you're an independent contractor and can be held liable to your client if there's a problem with the work you've done. When you were an employee, you didn't face this kind of liability.

What will all this mean to you? If you have not incorporated your consulting business, you can be held personally liable for any damages that arise out of your consulting services. That means that the sheriff could seize as much of your personal assets as are needed to satisfy a judgment arising out of your business. This includes your bank accounts, your stocks and bonds, your house, and your automobiles.

Note that, in general, all of your personal assets are at risk to satisfy a personal judgment against you. However, certain assets may be exempt from creditors under state and federal law, such as pensions, a portion of the equity of your house, and life insurance policies. The specific exemptions vary from state to state.

However, if you had been operating your consulting business as a corporation or other entity of limited liability, then the entity would be liable and not you personally. The assets of the entity could be seized to satisfy a judgment against the business, but your house, your savings, and all of your other personal assets would be safe. Incorporating your business provides a protection from personal liability for the debts and other obligations of the business. Operating without this protection, on the other hand, exposes all of your personal assets to the risks associated with your business.

Strategic Alliances and Potential Liability

In today's world of virtual offices and the like, consultants often join together in strategic alliances to provide a broader package of services to their clients. A typical strategic alliance may, for instance, consist of a product design consultant, a financial consultant, a consumer products consultant, and a market research consultant, each of whom provide complementary services in the same niche market. In order to present a broader range of services to their clients, these consultants may join together to market their expertise as a complete package of services geared to the development and marketing of specialty consumer products. To enhance this joint marketing, the group may adopt a group name, group letterhead, group advertising, and central billing for their group clients. Each individual consultant maintains his or her own individual consulting practice, but they join together from time to time for specific projects.

Assume that you are the market research consultant in this strategic alliance that you call the Orion Marketing Group. The group is successful in marketing its services and has been retained by a client to provide market research and development services for a new type of disposable diaper. Each of you is responsible for providing the specific services within your area of expertise, and the final product will be a complete market research and development study for the proposed new product.

Upon completion of this project, you furnish the client with the completed study. But after launching its new product, your client is very disappointed in the results. It is a total financial failure. The client's treasurer, eager to find a scapegoat for this financial fiasco, looks back at the study that your group performed. After a thorough investigation, it turns out that the financial projections contained in your study were faulty. The financial consultant in your strategic alliance relied on out-of-date information to prepare the financial projections. When this is uncovered, fingers are pointed. And they're pointed at you and at each of the other consultants in the group, not just at the financial consultant.

"How could I possibly be liable for the financial consultant's mistakes?" you exclaim. "I don't know the first thing about numbers. I'm only responsible for the market research end of these services. This has to be some kind of joke."

Even though you didn't handle the financial projections, you may well find yourself personally liable for the faulty financial information contained in your group's study. Your client may claim that you and the other members of Orion are partners in a general partnership. In support of the claim that your strategic alliance constituted a general partnership, your client can point to your Orion letterhead, Orion billing, Orion advertising, and your other efforts reflecting the joint packaging of your services.

If the group is deemed to be a general partnership, then each of the group members will be held jointly and severally liable for the debts and obligations of the enterprise. That means that you can be held personally liable if a judgment is rendered against the group.

Keep in mind that, even though you and the other members of Orion didn't intend to create a general partnership, a partnership relationship can be implied at law. All of those marketing techniques that you employed to present yourselves as a collaborative group of service providers will provide evidence that you were holding yourselves out to the public as a general partnership. As a result, you may be deemed to be operating as a general partnership. And if the group is deemed to be a general partnership, then each of the group members can be held jointly and severally liable for the obligations of the enterprise. That means that you can be held personally liable for the entire amount of the damages suffered by your client.

As you can see from this example, if you provide consulting services jointly with other consultants on a project basis, you face potential liability for a mistake made by one of the other consultants, whether or not you had any personal responsibility for those faulty services. Remember that if your consulting business has not been structured to protect you, then your personal assets will be exposed to satisfy this liability. However, if your consulting business is structured as a corporation, or other entity of limited liability, then it is the entity and not you personally that would face liability for the mistakes of your partners.

General Contract Liability

You will be entering into many types of contracts in your consulting business. In addition to entering into contracts with your clients, you will be contracting with the people who supply you with goods and services for your business. Contracts with your suppliers include your office lease if you are renting business space; your equipment leases if you are leasing a fax machine, photocopier, or other equipment; your advertising agreements — you mean to say your Yellow Pages representative hasn't contacted you yet? — your business insurance policies; and so on. As will be discussed in Chapter 4, a contract need not be in writing to be enforceable. In other words, you may be entering into contracts on a handshake or over the telephone without even realizing it.

Each and every contract you enter into will impose obligations on you, an obligation to pay money, perhaps, or an obligation to provide specified consulting services. If you fail to satisfy your obligations under any of these contracts, you can be held liable for damages. This means that you can be forced by a court to pay money to the other party to compensate them for the damages they suffered as a result of your breach.

If you are not operating as a corporation or other entity of limited liability, then you will be held personally liable for these damages. If you had formed a corporation or other entity of limited liability, then your business entity would be liable but you would not have any personal liability for breach of contract. Here are some examples of general contractual liability.

Contractual Liability under a Lease

Assume that you've decided to work outside of the home. Perhaps the dog barking or the baby crying does not lend quite the right degree of professional decorum you'd like for your new business. You will be entering into a lease with the landlord which will require that you pay the rent during the entire term of the lease. Say that you sign a three-year lease and that one year into the lease you decide the consulting business just wasn't right for you. You'd like to shut down the business, but you still have two years left on your lease.

If you had formed a corporation or other entity of limited liability and that entity was the tenant, then it is the entity and not you personally that would be liable for breach of the lease. A judgment against the entity could be satisfied out of the entity's assets such as bank accounts, receivables, or other property, but your assets would be protected. This example assumes that you have not personally guaranteed the lease. See Chapter 3 for a discussion of personal guarantees.

This is not to say that you should go into business planning to default on your contractual obligations. Nor should you treat lightly the obligations you undertake in your business dealings. But circumstances can change. You may fully intend to satisfy your obligations when you enter into a contract, but then something happens and you find that you are not able to fulfill your obligations. A major client may shift its business away from you, making a serious dent in your cash flow. Or a client may default on their payment obligations to you, leaving you unable to pay your own creditors. In an extreme case, your client may file for bankruptcy protection, leaving you with a large and probably uncollectible receivable.

For any number of reasons, you may be unable to satisfy your contractual obligations. By structuring your business appropriately, you can protect your personal assets from exposure for these liabilities.

Contractual Liability When You Least Expect It

When you enter into a lease or other written contract, you do it with your eyes open, knowing that you are obligating yourself to perform. But you may also find yourself obligated on a contract that you didn't even know you'd entered into. Here is an example.

Assume that you're in the business of organizing conferences for insurance companies. Because it seems simplest, you're operating as a sole proprietor. You'd been doing this kind of work in-house for a number of years, but your former employer and many other insurance companies are now contracting out this type of work. You're working with a new client, ABC Insurance Company, organizing their annual agents' convention for which you've booked conference facilities and 75 rooms at the Atlanta Hilton. Unfortunately, relations deteriorate with this client several weeks before the convention, and you both agree to terminate your relationship. You move on to bigger and better projects without giving another thought to the ABC Insurance Company.

Then you receive a bill from the Atlanta Hilton several months later for 25 of the rooms that you'd previously booked for the ABC Insurance Company. It seems that turnout wasn't as high as expected at their annual convention. Only 50 agents came to the conference, and no one had thought to cancel the extra room reservations. The Atlanta Hilton is threatening to sue you for breach of contract if you don't pay the outstanding balance of $10,000.

Of course you'll say that it's the ABC Insurance Company that should be liable for those rooms and not you. But you're the one who booked those rooms and confirmed the reservation with your personal credit card, and it's your name and address that are reflected as the booking party on the hotel's records. You are now facing contractual liability that could wipe out all of your earnings for the past quarter, and you didn't even know you'd entered into a contract.

Clearly there are two sides to this story, and you could well prevail in the lawsuit when the Hilton sues you. But to do so you'll have to pay a lawyer to defend you. And you'll need to spend a significant amount of time preparing for your day in court, which means that you'll have less time available for your productive business.

As a sole proprietor, all of your personal assets are exposed to satisfy your business obligations, so you've got to do all you can to defend yourself. If, however, you had been operating as a corporation or other entity of limited liability, the Hilton could sue your entity but not you personally. Yes, the corporate assets would be exposed, but your personal assets would be safe.

As these examples show, to protect yourself against personal liability arising out of contractual obligations, your best bet is to operate as a corporation or other entity of limited liability. If you don't, you're exposing all of your personal assets to the risks of your business.

Employer Liability

In the anecdote at the beginning of this chapter, you may recall that Jim faces liability because his employee had an auto accident and hit a bicyclist on his way to the client's office. Jim wasn't driving, he wasn't even in the car, and yet he is being sued by the bicyclist. How can this be? It's surprisingly simple. Jim, as an employer, is liable for his employees' actions so long as those actions are within the scope of their employment. This kind of liability is well-established in the law. It even has a very dignified sounding Latin name: *respondeat superior*, which literally means let the master answer.

The employer's liability for the acts of his employee is a no-fault liability. In other words, it is in no way based on any wrongful conduct of the employer. Instead, it is based on a public policy rationale that the business should bear the risk of the wrongful acts of its agents or employees. One reason for this risk allocation is the assumption that businesses have deep pockets and will therefore be able to pay for any injuries caused by their employees.

What relevance does all this Latin-sounding liability have to you and your consulting business? As your business expands, you may be hiring employees to help in your consulting business. Hopefully, demand for your services will be so great that you'll be forced to bring others on board to help out. By hiring employees, you are exposing yourself to liability for their acts, acts on the job as well as acts associated with their job, like Bill's accident on the way to his client's office.

As an employer, you can be held liable for any and all acts of your employees that are within the scope of their duties. You have just looked at a simple example of employer liability, an employee who is in a car accident on the way to visit a client. In today's workplace, potential employer liability can lurk in every corner. What about the employee who charges another employee with sexual harassment? Or the programmer who claims to have been fired, or not hired, because of his or her race or gender or mental disability?

It's clear that employer liability can be a risk in any business today. Is it a risk you're prepared to ignore? If not, your best protection is a corporation or other entity of limited liability.

Partnership Liability

You have already taken a look at the potential liability of the members of a strategic alliance who, without realizing it, may be deemed to be general partners in a partnership. Even in instances when the individuals know that they are operating as a partnership, unexpected liability can result. Here is a simple example.

Jack and his best friend, Gary, have joined forces to open a payroll consulting business, Paymasters Company. They've been friends since grade school and always dreamed of starting a business together. Jack's background is in payroll processing, and Gary is a born salesman, a perfect combination to start their own payroll processing and consulting business. They provide advice to businesses who want to set up a computerized in-house payroll system. They also provide a payroll service for businesses who can't be bothered to handle it themselves. The doors have been open for just over two years, and business has been good.

Jack and Gary couldn't be bothered to incorporate and never bothered to have any kind of partnership agreement drawn up. "After all," they said, "we're like brothers. Why do we need all kinds of legal papers?" Jack and Gary confer on all major business decisions like marketing strategies, employee staffing, and major purchases. Gary is more aggressive in his plans for the business than Jack, but for the most part, they're in general agreement.

Gary is taking his first real vacation since they started the business. He's in California touring the wine country when he happens upon a close-out sale of floor-model computers. They really need to upgrade their existing computers anyway, and the prices are so good that Gary can't resist ordering ten computers with monitors and printers. Even though they don't need all ten computers right now, Gary is sure that their business will be growing so fast that they'll need them soon. Maybe the wine tasting he'd just been to helped to color Gary's business judgment a little. He tries to call Jack to talk it over with him, but Jack is out on the road all day and can't be reached. He's sure that Jack will agree with him and, not wanting to pass up a bargain, Gary signs the purchase agreement as a partner in Paymasters Company. The total purchase price with shipping and handling is $20,000, which the seller is financing at an interest rate of 18 percent.

The computers arrive at the office shortly after Gary gets back from vacation, but Gary is so busy he doesn't bother to unpack them and ships them off to storage. Unfortunately, the business didn't expand as much as Gary expected. In fact, business hit a serious downturn, and within six months Jack and Gary decide to close up the business. Gary decides to open a sports bar on some slow-paced Caribbean Island, and Jack goes back to work as a bookkeeper. Before long, Jack is being served with a lawsuit for the balance due on the computers that Gary had bought out in sunny California.

This is the first Jack has even heard about these computers, and he's certain that he can't be liable to pay this debt. Think again, Jack. Whether they knew it or not, Gary and Jack were operating as partners in a general partnership. As partners, each of them is liable, jointly and severally, for all obligations of the partnership. That means a creditor of the partnership can recover his full debt from either partner. In this example, the computer seller is not limited to recovering one-half of the debt from Jack. He can recover the entire debt from Jack. The fact that Gary ordered these computers without Jack's permission or even knowledge does not relieve Jack from liability for the debt. Provided that this purchase was within the usual business of the partnership, Gary's purchase is binding on the partnership and on each of the partners individually.

If Jack is forced to pay the entire partnership debt, he will have a right of contribution against his partner. This means that if Jack pays $20,000 to satisfy his debt, he can recover $10,000 from Gary — if and when he can find him.

This example illustrates one of the risks of operating as a general partnership. Each partner is personally liable for the obligations of the partnership, even if he or she didn't know about the transaction. If Gary and Jack had been operating as a corporation or other entity of limited liability, then neither one of them would have faced personal liability for this obligation.

Premises Liability

If someone trips on the steps in front of your house, you may well be sued for negligence. If your guest is injured, they may claim that you were negligent in failing to properly maintain the steps. Perhaps they tripped on a loose board or slid on some ice. If they were injured as a result of your negligence, then you will be liable for their damages. Of course, that's why your homeowner's insurance policy or renter's policy includes liability coverage.

The same type of potential liability exists in operating your business. If someone is injured on your business premises as a result of your negligence, you can be held liable for their injuries. In this instance, negligence is the failure to take reasonable steps to keep your business premises safe. Every business faces this type of potential liability which is referred to as premises liability. However, by operating as a corporation or other entity of limited liability, this liability would attach to your entity and not to you personally.

Take note that if you're operating your consulting business out of your home and an accident occurs in connection with your business, don't try to rely on your homeowner's or renter's insurance. These policies typically exclude liability arising out of the operation of a trade or business from the home. Check with your insurance agent about getting a rider to your policy to cover your home-based business. It shouldn't cost more than a few hundred dollars.

Every consultant should look closely at his or her business to identify the areas of potential liability associated with that particular business. Don't be lulled into a false sense of security just because you're operating your consulting business out of your home. A million-dollar judgment can be rendered against a consultant whether they operate out of a downtown office building or out of a home office.

Unanticipated Liability

No matter how thorough you are in assessing the potential liabilities associated with your consulting business, you can always be stung by the oops factor. This is the liability exposure that just didn't come to mind when you were calmly weighing the risks associated with your business. Maybe it's an oversight on your part, or maybe it's a new kind of liability that wasn't even around when you first started your business. People who started their business 15 years ago didn't give any thought to potential liability for sexual harassment or non-compliance with the Americans with Disabilities Act, for example. These areas of liability result from newly-enacted statutes.

Whatever potential liabilities your business may face, operating as a corporation or other entity of limited liability will provide you and your personal assets with the maximum available protection. Operating as a sole proprietorship or as a partnership may, at first glance, seem simpler than incorporating, but remember that doing so puts all of your personal assets at risk. Is that something you can feel comfortable with?

Which of these areas of potential liability will you face in your consulting business?

- Liability arising out of a client's dissatisfaction with your consulting services.
- Liability for mistakes of others in your strategic alliance.
- Liability under contracts with suppliers.
- Liability for the acts of your employees.
- Liability for actions taken by your partner, with or without your knowledge.
- Liability for what happens at your business premises.
- Liability created by new statutes.

If you're convinced that you want to obtain the maximum protection from personal liability, read on to find out which entity of limited liability will work best for you.

Chapter 2

A Corporation, LLC, or LLP

Which One Is Right for You?

You're ready to open your own consulting business. You've got some retirement money saved up that you're prepared to risk on the venture. You've got your home office set up with a computer, fax, and answering machine. You're all set to go except for choosing the type of business entity. And it seems that everyone you know wants to help you with this decision. Your cousin Victor, who's been in business for 20 years, says that an S corporation is the way to go. Your sister-in-law Sally, who used to be married to an accountant, tells you that the LLC is right for you. A look at your bank balance makes you wonder if it's worth forming any entity when you could operate as a sole proprietor and save all those legal and accounting fees.

As you know by now, unless you form a corporation or other entity of limited liability, you are exposing yourself to personal liability for the risks of your business. One of the main reasons to form a corporation or other entity of limited liability is to protect your personal assets. But you will also need to consider the tax consequences that will result from your choice of a business entity.

In this chapter, you'll take a look at corporations, the more traditional route for the small business owner seeking limited liability. You'll also take a look at the new kid on the block, the limited liability company. By the time you've finished reading this chapter, you'll be prepared to make a rational and well informed decision. You didn't really feel comfortable relying on business advice from cousin Victor or sister-in-law Sally, now did you?

Which Kind of Corporation?

You deal with corporations every day of your life. Maybe it's a big corporation like AT&T trying to convince you to change long distance carriers. Maybe you're picking up clothes at your dry cleaner, Redi-Clean, Inc., or having your muffler changed at Redi-Muffler, Inc. Corporations are a big part of people's lives.

You may be wondering what your little consulting business could possibly have in common with AT&T. If you decide to form a corporation, your form of business entity will be exactly the same as AT&T's. You don't have to be a mega-business to operate as a corporation. Even a small business like yours can incorporate and obtain the same protection from personal liability as a corporate conglomerate.

The primary reason that any business incorporates, whether the business is big or small, is to protect its owners from personal liability. The owners of a corporation are not personally liable for the debts and other obligations of the corporation. Their potential loss is limited to the amount invested in the business.

Read on for a brief overview of the legal structure of a corporation that will also take some of the mystery out of basic corporate terminology.

Structure of a Corporation

A corporation is comprised of shareholders, directors, and officers. The shareholders invest the capital in the corporation and are the owners of the corporation. As shareholders, they are entitled to receive dividends if and when authorized by the board of directors. Also, upon dissolution of the corporation, the shareholders are entitled to receive a liquidating distribution of all the corporation's net assets, following payment of the corporation's debts. Shareholders have little control over the day-to-day operations of the corporation. Their primary responsibility is to elect the directors of the corporation.

The directors of the corporation are responsible for making the policy decisions for the company. The directors will vote, for instance, on whether the company will take out a working capital loan. The directors are also responsible for appointing the officers of the corporation. It is the officers of the corporation who oversee the day-to-day operations of the business. The most common officers are the president, treasurer, and secretary.

If you form a corporation for your consulting business, you may well wear a number of different hats within your corporation. You may be the sole owner of the corporation, that is, its sole shareholder. As the sole shareholder, you may elect yourself the sole director of the corporation. And as the sole director, you may appoint yourself as president of the corporation. This may seem a bit confusing at first, but remember that, in structure, your corporation is no different from AT&T. It's just that a smaller number of people, and maybe only one person, serve in these various roles.

If you do chose to operate your consulting business as a corporation, you must make sure your corporation is properly formed. Because a corporation is a creature of statute, the requirements of the governing statutes must be strictly complied with; otherwise, the corporation will not legally exist, and you will face personal liability for the obligations of the business. One of the simplest ways of ensuring that your corporation is properly formed is to rely on the expertise of a competent small business attorney. Later, in Chapter 7 you will read about the importance of working with an attorney experienced in representing small businesses.

A corporation is formed under the laws of a particular state, and if a corporation transacts business in other states, it is required to qualify to do business in those other states by filing the necessary paperwork in those states.

You may be considering incorporating your business under the laws of Delaware because you've heard that Delaware corporations are the best. It's true that Delaware law is particularly favorable to businesses. If you're planning to sell stock to the public or engage in hostile takeover bids, you probably should consider incorporating in Delaware. But if your business will stay closely held, then you don't need all the bells and whistles provided by a Delaware corporation, and you're better off incorporating in the state where you'll be doing business. For one thing, it will cost you less. Remember that if you incorporate in Delaware and transact business in your home state, you will also need to qualify to do business in your home state. That means two sets of filing fees every year. Also, the filing fees in your home state for a corporation that is formed under the laws of another state are usually substantially higher than the fees for an in-state corporation.

Tax Treatment of a C Corporation

A corporation, once formed, is a separate legal entity. It is also a separate taxable entity, taxable under Subchapter C of the Internal Revenue Code, hence the term C corporation. A corporation will have its own federal and state taxpayer identification numbers and will be required to file corporate tax returns.

One of the disadvantages of the corporation is that its net earnings are subject to double taxation, first as income to the corporation, then as dividends to the shareholders. A corporation pays income tax based on its net taxable income which, in simple terms, is equal to its gross income less all deductible business expenses. Then when the corporation distributes its net after-tax profits to its shareholders, the shareholders pay personal income tax on that dividend income. This is often referred to as the double taxation of corporate profits. Look at a simple example to see how this works.

Assume that you form a corporation you call At Your Service, Inc., or AYS. In its first fiscal year, AYS has collected $125,000 in gross income. Business expenses for the year, including your salary, total $100,000. The annual net profit of AYS is $25,000. On this profit, the corporation will pay federal as well as state corporate income tax. For purposes of this example, assume that the combined corporate tax bite is 20 percent.

Therefore, of the $25,000 in net profit, AYS will pay $5,000 in corporate tax. If the remaining balance of $20,000 is distributed as a dividend to you as the sole shareholder, the dividend payment will not be deductible by the corporation and you as the shareholder will pay personal income tax on that dividend income. The personal income tax paid by the shareholder will be a function of the shareholder's marginal tax rate.

In the summary chart below, the sole shareholder's marginal tax rate is 30 percent. You can see from this example the impact of the double taxation of corporate profits.

C Corporation Taxation

Annual gross income	$125,000
Deductible business expenses	−100,000
Annual net income	25,000
Federal and state corporate taxes	−5,000
Net after-tax income to corporation	20,000
Dividend distributed to shareholder	20,000
Personal income taxes @ 30%	−6,000
Net after-tax income to shareholder	$ 14,000

Keep in mind that your corporate income tax is computed on the basis of the corporation's net taxable income and that there are ways of reducing the net taxable income. For instance, the directors of the corporation may decide to award you a year-end bonus to compensate you for your hard work during the year. In this way, the additional compensation, provided that it is reasonable, will be deductible by the corporation and will reduce the corporation's net taxable income. This, in turn, will reduce the corporate tax payable by the corporation. Of course, you will be paying personal income tax on the bonus you receive from the corporation. The bonus income, however, will be subject to only one level of taxation instead of two.

A good business accountant can help you review the corporation's finances prior to its fiscal year end to assist you in minimizing the impact of double taxation of corporate profits.

The S Corporation, a Corporation That Pays No Income Tax

Wouldn't it be great if you could operate as a corporation without the headache of double taxation? Believe it or not, the IRS allows certain qualifying corporations to do just that. If a corporation meets certain criteria, it can file an election with the IRS to be taxed under Subchapter S of the Internal Revenue Code. The restrictions imposed on an S corporation include a limit on the number of shareholders, recently increased to 75, as well as on the type of shareholders.

An S corporation is treated like a partnership for federal income tax purposes. This means that there is no income tax payable to the IRS at the corporate level. Instead, the corporation's income or loss is passed through to the shareholders. The shareholders report their share of the corporation's income or loss on their personal tax returns. While the corporation is required to file an informational return with the IRS, there is no federal income tax payable by the corporation.

It is important to remember that an S corporation is no different from other corporations in its legal structure. What makes an S corporation different is the filing of a one-page form with the IRS to elect to be taxed under Subchapter S of the Internal Revenue Code.

Take another look at that AYS corporate tax example but now assuming that AYS is an S corporation.

S Corporation Taxation

Annual gross income	$125,000
Deductible business expenses	−100,000
Annual net income	25,000
Federal and state corporate taxes	−0
Net after-tax income to corporation	25,000
Income distributed to shareholder	25,000
Personal income taxes @ 30%	−8,333
Net after-tax income to shareholder	$ 16,667

As you can see from this example, the total taxes payable if AYS were a C corporation would be $11,000, leaving net after-tax income to the shareholder of $14,000. If AYS were an S corporation, the total taxes payable would be $8,333, leaving net after-tax income to the shareholder of $16,667. You can see why so many small businesses elect Subchapter S status for their corporations.

The S corporation thus eliminates the potential for double taxation of corporate profits. But be careful. There are a number of states that do not recognize Subchapter S status for purposes of determining state corporate income tax. If you are doing business in such a state, your S corporation will be liable for state corporate income tax if it shows a net taxable profit. And even if your S corporation does not show a net taxable profit, you may still be required to pay the state's minimum corporate tax. Check with your accountant to see whether an S corporation is an option for you in your state.

Hurrah for the Limited Liability Company

Throughout this book, the importance of protecting yourself by forming a corporation or other entity of limited liability has been emphasized. What are these other entities of limited liability? Besides the corporation, other business entities that provide protection from personal liability include the limited partnership, limited liability partnership, and the limited liability company. Don't be confused by the similarity in their names because each one is a very different kind of legal entity. For a consulting business such as yours, the limited liability company (LLC) could well be the right choice for you. Take a look first at the new kid on the block, the LLC.

Overview of the LLC

The limited liability company combines the limited liability benefits of a corporation with the pass-through tax advantages of a partnership. Because of its limited liability feature, the owners of the LLC are not personally liable for the debts or other obligations of the LLC. Their potential loss is limited to the amount invested in the business. Because of its pass-through tax benefits, the owners will not face the double taxation associated with a corporation. Although a relatively new kind of business entity, now that the LLC has been adopted in all 50 states, it is sure to become the entity of choice for many small businesses.

Unlike the formal legal structure of a corporation, an LLC is a more flexible kind of business entity. Unlike a corporation, there are no shareholders, directors or officers of an LLC. Instead, the owners of an LLC are called its members. The members enter into an operating agreement which provides the framework for the operation of the LLC. The operating agreement is very much like a partnership agreement. It identifies the percentage ownership interest held by each member and addresses operational issues such as the vote required to authorize LLC action and how much money the members will contribute to the LLC. In addition, the operating agreement should contain other provisions including a mechanism to buy out the interest of a deceased, disabled, or retiring member.

The limited liability company grows out of the law of partnership. Like partners in a partnership, each member of an LLC is deemed to be an agent of the LLC and can take actions to bind the LLC. But in this regard there's one major difference between a partnership and an LLC. If a partner undertakes an obligation on behalf of a partnership, not only is the partnership liable for that obligation, each and every partner is also personally liable for that obligation. This is true even if the other partners did not consent to their partner taking the action. In contrast, if a member of an LLC undertakes an obligation on behalf of the LLC, it is the LLC that will be liable for such obligation. Because of the shelter from personal liability afforded to members of an LLC, the individual members will not be personally liable for that obligation.

The members can appoint one or more managers to run the LLC, vesting as much or as little authority as they choose in the managers. If the LLC is run by one or more managers, then the members are no longer deemed to be agents of the LLC and only the managers can legally take action on behalf of the LLC.

The LLC is a terrific form of business entity and may be just right for your consulting business. But be careful because it is not suitable for everyone. For one thing, in some states, to be taxed as a pass-through entity, the LLC must have at least two members, although the second member can own as little as one percent of the company. In addition, there may be other tax reasons why a corporation may be better for you.

Other Tax Consequences

Besides looking at the different ways in which profits are taxed in a corporation and an LLC, keep in mind that there are other tax consequences that can have a significant impact on your choice of a business entity. These can include, for example, deductibility of group health insurance premiums by the business and the availability of certain tax-sheltered retirement plans. Because this is a complicated and ever-changing area of the tax law, it is essential that you obtain the advice of a good business accountant in choosing a form of business entity.

Other Entities of Limited Liability

Another commonly known entity of limited liability is the limited partnership. Because of the pass-through tax benefits it provides, the limited partnership was a popular vehicle for real estate ventures, particularly real estate syndications. The main drawback of the limited partnership is the requirement that there be at least one general partner who has personal liability for all obligations of the limited partnership. While the family limited partnership can be valuable as an estate planning tool, the limited partnership has limited value today for small business.

A number of states have adopted statutes permitting a partnership to operate as a limited liability partnership (LLP). The liability of the partners in an LLP is limited in accordance with the particular state's statute. In some states, the LLP can provide the same kind of protection from liability as a corporation or LLC. But in other states, the protection is limited and may exclude, for instance, protection against contractual obligations of the entity. Another drawback of the LLP is the lack of protection in states that have not adopted an LLP statute, which currently is about one-third of the states. An LLP operating in a non-LLP state will not afford any protection from personal liability to its owners.

For further information about setting up or converting to an LLC, consult *The Essential Limited Liability Company Handbook: The Newest Alternative in Business*, by Corporate Agents, Inc. This helpful book, published by The Oasis Press, is written in layperson language and includes a sample operating agreement as well as LLC requirements for the 50 states and the District of Columbia.

Go Out There and Make a Million

Now that you've had a close look at the business entities available to you, don't you feel well-informed and able to make a rational business decision? When you meet with your lawyer about forming your business entity, you should be well prepared to understand his or her advice. If not, maybe you haven't chosen the right lawyer to assist you.

Chapter 3

Some Words of Wisdom
About Operating Your Business

In the earlier chapters you read about the types of liability you can face as a consultant. These include potential liability for your consulting services, contract liability, and partnership liability, to name a few. You then looked at the tremendous benefits you can achieve by operating your business as a corporation or other entity of limited liability. But keep in mind that forming a corporation, LLC, or other business entity is no substitute for maintaining adequate liability insurance against the particular risks associated with your business. In this chapter you'll learn about the importance of maintaining liability insurance to protect you and your business.

It's important to understand that there are certain areas of potential liability that no business entity can protect you against. Even if you operate as a corporation or other entity of limited liability, you may face personal liability for debts owed by your business to the Internal Revenue Service. Also, if your business faces liability for environmental contamination, you may well face personal liability for the clean-up costs. This chapter reviews areas of liability for which your entity will not provide you protection.

Even if you form a corporation or LLC, you will still face personal liability for debts of the business if you personally guarantee these debts.

Often in a start-up business, the owners are required by creditors to personally guarantee specific business obligations such as a lease or business loan. Later in this chapter you'll look at personal guarantees and ways of limiting your exposure under guarantees.

Lastly, keep in mind that it's not enough to form a corporation or other entity of limited liability. You must comply with all of the legal formalities required of that business entity. Otherwise, you may well find yourself facing personal liability for the business obligations under a common law doctrine known as piercing the corporate veil. At the end of this chapter you'll read about this area of potential personal liability including ways to minimize your exposure to it.

Liability Insurance

Every business has liability risks associated with it. In Chapter 1, you learned of the kinds of risk that you may face in operating your consulting business. No doubt you're convinced by now of the importance of forming an entity of limited liability to protect your personal assets against the risks associated with your business. Organizing your business in this way is not enough. You also need to make sure that you maintain adequate liability insurance to protect you and your business against insurable risks.

If you have automobile or homeowner's insurance, then you're probably familiar with the general principles of liability insurance. Your homeowner's insurance would, for instance, compensate someone who was injured on your property as a result of your carelessness. For example, if you left a rake on your front path and Violet Visitor tripped over it one dark night, Violet could make a claim against you for her medical bills and other damages resulting from her injuries. If you owed her money because of this accident, your insurance company would pay that money on your behalf. In addition, your insurance company would pay the cost of defending you in a lawsuit if Violet ended up suing you.

As a consultant, you may face negligence liability in a number of areas. An area of potential liability common to all businesses is premises liability.

If clients or anyone else visit your business premises, you run the risk that they will be injured on your premises as a result of your negligence. Think of yourself as the supermarket owner with customers wandering up and down the aisles and a slippery banana peel just waiting to cause an accident. To protect yourself and your business against this kind of risk, you need to maintain adequate liability insurance.

Another kind of insurance that you should look into is errors and omissions insurance, often referred to as E&O or professional liability coverage. This insurance provides coverage for services negligently performed. It is similar to the malpractice insurance that doctors and lawyers maintain. If, for instance, one of your clients threatened to sue you because of poor workmanship in performing consulting services, this claim would be covered by your E&O insurance. Check with your insurance agent to find out about purchasing this kind of insurance.

To make sure that you've got all the information you need about business insurance, it's best to work with an insurance agent who really knows about the needs of small business owners. Explain your business to the agent and find out exactly what kind of liability insurance is available to suit your particular needs.

At this point, you may be wondering why you should bother to form an entity of limited liability if you will be maintaining adequate liability insurance. To protect yourself, you need to incorporate and maintain adequate liability insurance. First, there are plenty of business risks out there which are uninsurable. Liability insurance won't, for instance, protect you against a breach of contract claim. Insurance is great for what it provides, but it is by no means all-encompassing. Second, your insurance will have a deductible component which is the amount that you are required to pay out of pocket. In addition, your insurance will have a maximum dollar coverage and you will face liability for any amount in excess of the policy amount. Last, it can sometimes be difficult to convince an insurance company to pay out on a claim even if it is covered under the policy. Just imagine some clerk in your insurance company whose sole job it is to wield a big red stamp and mark all claims that come across their desk as claim denied.

You can see, therefore, how important it is to maintain adequate liability insurance appropriate to the needs of your particular business.

Collect Sales Tax if Applicable

In some states, consulting services are subject to state sales tax. Make sure you check with your accountant to find out if your consulting services are subject to sales tax in the states where you do business. If your services are subject to sales tax, be sure to collect the tax from your clients in addition to your consulting fees. If your clients balk at paying sales tax, tell them it's just like buying a candy bar in the drug store. The price tag is marked 50 cents, but the cashier collects 53 cents to include the tax.

Don't rely on what your consulting colleagues tell you about sales tax. Just because your colleagues aren't charging sales tax doesn't mean that they're not required to pay sales tax on their consulting income. It may only mean they haven't been audited yet.

Other Legal Requirements

Licensing and permit requirements vary widely from state to state and even from one town to another. Check to make sure that you have any state or local licenses that are required for your consulting services. For assistance in obtaining this information, see the Consultants' Resource Directory in Appendix D.

If you do decide to operate your consulting business as a sole proprietor or partnership, you may be required to file a fictitious name certificate. If, for instance, John Smith is a sole proprietor using the name Ace Software Consulting for his business, he would need to file a fictitious name certificate in his local registry office disclosing that he is operating under that business name.

Also if you're operating your consulting business out of your home, make sure that you're not in violation of local zoning laws. You can usually get a copy of the zoning laws from your local town hall or county registry office. There may be limitations on certain business uses of your home, including restrictions on parking, business signs, and access by the general public. In addition, if you live in a condominium or other planned community, be sure to check your community's rules and regulations. Similarly, if you rent your home or apartment and plan to use it as a home office, check your lease to see if there are any restrictions on a business use of the property.

No Entity Protects from All Liability

Hopefully, you're convinced about the benefits of forming an entity of limited liability. To give you the full picture, however, you've got to be told the sad truth. There are some kinds of liability that no entity can protect you against.

IRS Trust Fund Taxes

If your business is required to collect withholding, social security taxes, or the like on behalf of your employees, then make extra sure that these taxes are, in fact, paid to the IRS. These kind of taxes are called trust fund taxes, and the IRS takes them very seriously. If a business fails to pay over these taxes to the IRS, then the IRS can impose personal liability on anyone and everyone in the business who should have forwarded that money to the IRS. You can rest assured that the IRS will cast a very large net in imposing personal liability on members of the business if the trust fund taxes have not been paid. And to top it off, you can't even escape these kinds of taxes by filing bankruptcy. The moral of the story is: pay them.

Chapter 5 will give you a more detailed explanation of the employer's withholding obligations.

Environmental Liability

Remember the general principle that the owners of a corporation or LLC are not personally liable for the obligations of the entity? That century-old principle has been turned on its head in the area of environmental liability. Federal environmental laws impose personal liability for clean-up costs on owners, operators, and practically anyone else who ever set foot on a contaminated property. In a small, closely held business, the principals are likely to face personal liability for any environmental clean-up costs imposed by governmental authorities. Unfortunately, because of the tremendous potential clean-up costs involved, it is difficult, if not impossible, to obtain insurance to protect you against environmental liability.

Personal Guarantees

If you've tried to get a bank loan for your start-up business, you probably know that most banks will not make a loan to a new business unless the owners are willing to personally guarantee the debt. So don't be surprised if you are asked to put up your house or other personal assets as security for a business loan for your start-up business. Similarly, if you will be leasing business premises, your landlord may request you to personally guarantee the lease. In either case, you have the option of saying no. You may find it difficult to obtain financing from a bank without a personal guarantee in the early stages of your business. If you are willing to shop around, however, you may be able to find a landlord who will not require a personal guarantee.

Even if you do decide to guarantee a business obligation, you can try to limit your exposure. You can propose to your creditor that your personal guarantee be limited to a specific dollar amount or to a specified period of time. After all, a guarantee is no more or less than a form of contract and, like other contracts, it can be freely negotiated by the parties.

Piercing the Corporate Veil

Forming a corporation or an LLC will provide you with significant protection from personal liability. However, it is not enough to simply form an entity of limited liability. It is essential that you keep thorough corporate records and maintain the legal and financial integrity of your new business. Otherwise, a creditor may be able to pierce the corporate veil which would expose you to unlimited personal liability for the obligations of the business. Unfortunately, there are no black-and-white rules that govern this area of the law. Piercing the corporate veil is a doctrine that has grown up over the years on a case-by-case basis. Basically, it is the result applied when a judge or jury concludes that the business owners did something so bad that they shouldn't be permitted to hide behind the corporate shield.

The kinds of factors that will affect a decision to pierce the corporate veil include co-mingled personal and corporate assets, inadequate operating capital, and inattention to legal formalities. The following is a list of practical pointers which not only make good business sense but will also help you avoid personal liability under the doctrine of piercing the corporate, or LLC, veil.

- Maintain a separate bank account that is in the name of your business and is used only for valid business purposes.
- Make sure you operate your business with adequate working capital.
- Maintain adequate liability insurance for the particular risks associated with your business.
- Always present yourself as a corporation or LLC on all of your stationery, business cards, and advertising materials.
- Always sign contracts on behalf of your entity and not individually. They should be signed, for instance, as: XYZ, Inc., by John Smith, its president.
- Maintain your corporate books and records. It is particularly important if you have formed a corporation to hold shareholders' and directors' meetings at least once a year and include a record of these meetings in your minute book.
- Make sure that you make all the necessary filings with government agencies to maintain your legal existence.
- Do not allow your business to be used to commit fraud.

The Essential Corporation Handbook by Carl R.J. Sniffen, published by The Oasis Press, contains detailed information about record keeping and the other things required to keep your corporation or LLC in good standing.

Chapter 4

Oral Contracts

Don't Get Burned

Sarah started her consulting business two years ago. An expert in total quality management (TQM), she provides TQM training to her corporate clients through her corporation TQM, Inc. Business had been growing at a slow but steady pace, and Sarah was thrilled to land a new client recently. She and the CEO of Alpha Corporation hit it off great, and Sarah was retained to provide a week-long TQM seminar at Alpha's headquarters. Sarah and the CEO shook hands on the deal and didn't bother to have their lawyers draw up a contract. When Sarah completed the work, she sent an invoice to the CEO and looked forward to receiving the $10,000 fee for her services.

Instead of a check, Sarah got a letter from the CEO stating that, per their agreement, Sarah was required to deliver all of her written training materials before Alpha would make any payment to her. "That wasn't our deal," Sarah complains to no one in particular. "I provided a week of TQM training for $10,000. I never agreed to turn over my training materials to Alpha. I've put years of work into developing those materials, and I'd never hand them over to a client." What started out as a promising long-term relationship with a new client is quickly turning into a potential lawsuit, and Sarah wonders if she'll ever see any money for her week of hard work.

Sarah made the mistake of doing business on a handshake. Sarah and the CEO entered into an agreement for consulting services which they did not bother to put down on paper. The problem arose because, as it turns out, Sarah and the CEO had very different ideas about the scope of the services that Sarah would be providing for that $10,000 fee. If they had put their agreement down on paper, this problem could have been avoided. Doing business on a handshake is a very dangerous practice. This chapter will discuss the importance of using written contracts.

What Is a Contract?

First, what is a contract? A contract is just the legal term for an agreement. When your lawyer hands you a long document titled Agreement and asks you to sign it before witnesses, it's clear that you are entering into a contract. But signing a document is not the only way you can enter into a contract. You can also enter into a contract orally without ever putting pen to paper.

A contract is the result of a simple two-step process of offer and acceptance. If you make an offer to provide goods or services to your client and your client accepts that offer, a contract has been formed. For instance, in Sarah's situation, Sarah offered to provide TQM services to Alpha, and Alpha accepted Sarah's offer. In this way, they entered into a contract even though it was not set down in a written agreement.

Here is another example of an oral contract. Your local newspaper sends a sales rep to suggest that you advertise your new business in their paper. You are impressed by their rates of $50 per week for a ten-week run. You hand your ad copy to the rep to run in the next ten editions. The sales rep thanks you for your business and leaves with your ad copy in hand.

It is likely that the sales rep will fax you a standard form advertising contract asking that you confirm the advertising terms by signing the contract. But even if you never sign a written contract with the newspaper, you and the newspaper are bound by the terms of the oral contract that you made. The newspaper offered to run your ad at $500 for a ten-week period, and you accepted that offer, so a contract has been formed. It's that easy.

Once you have entered into a contract, whether it's a written or an oral contract, you are each legally bound to fulfill your obligations under that contract. If you don't fulfill your obligations, then you are in breach of contract. And if that happens, you can be held liable to the other person for the damages suffered as a result of your breach.

In this example, if the newspaper runs your ad in the next ten editions, you will be obligated to pay the paper $500 in accordance with your verbal agreement. If you don't pay, then the newspaper can sue you to collect the money.

It is important to remember that, in general, a contract doesn't need to be in writing to be a legal and valid agreement. Except for certain kinds of agreements that are required by law to be in writing, the terms of an oral agreement are fully enforceable. In general, the kinds of agreements that are required to be in writing include an agreement to buy or sell real estate, an agreement to guarantee the debts of another, an agreement which is not to be fully performed within one year, and an agreement to buy or sell goods in excess of $500, or whatever dollar amount your state law provides. The laws of each state set forth which kinds of agreements are required to be in writing in a statute referred to as the Statute of Frauds. These statutes date back to the 1600s and were actually designed to prevent fraud.

For the most part, an agreement to provide consulting services is not required by law to be in writing. This means that you can enter into an enforceable consulting agreement without putting anything in writing. Be aware, however, that oral contracts can be very dangerous. When things go wrong, each party will tell a different story about what was agreed to. Without a written contract to refer to, proving the agreed-upon terms of that oral contract can be a real nightmare.

The Danger of Oral Contracts

For every consulting contract that you enter into with a client, there are only two possible outcomes. Either both of you are fully satisfied with the completed transaction or both of you are not fully satisfied with the completed transaction. Under this second outcome, the possibilities are that one or both of the parties are dissatisfied with the completed transaction. Certainly you hope that your business dealings fall into the first category. But it is important to take action to minimize the risk that they will fall into the second category. Documenting your agreements with a written contract is a simple and painless way to help your transactions stay within that blissful first category.

If you perform consulting services to the complete satisfaction of your client and your client pays your entire fee for these services in a timely manner, then you are both happy. Neither of you will be planning to hire a lawyer to sue the other for breach of contract. This transaction is clearly one that falls within the first category of possible outcomes in which both of you are fully satisfied with the completed transaction. In the end, it really didn't matter whether this agreement was done on a simple handshake or was reflected in a 20-page document.

Assume that things don't work out so well for you. Maybe your transaction is more like the example in the beginning of this chapter between Sarah and Alpha Corporation. In that example, Sarah performed consulting services but did not receive her fee. Clearly Sarah is not satisfied with Alpha's performance, their lack of payment. And it's quite possible that Alpha is dissatisfied with Sarah's performance, her failure to provide training materials. You have at least one, and quite probably two, parties who are dissatisfied.

Sarah will be hiring a lawyer to help her collect her fee. And that means that Alpha will be hiring a lawyer to defend against Sarah's claim. That situation will make for two very happy people, but they won't be Sarah and Alpha's CEO. They will be the two lawyers who will be earning large legal fees in dealing with this mess.

If you end up in a dispute with your client, you are in for some turbulence. But if you end up in a dispute with your client and you don't have a written contract, you'd better fasten your seat belt. With an oral contract, your lawyer will be arguing that the terms of the oral contract were X, and your opponent's lawyer will claim that the terms weren't X, that they were Y. However, without a written contract to turn to, it will be your word against theirs. Even if you prevail, you will have spent much time, energy, and money just to receive the fee you were entitled to anyway. If you lose, you'll have invested all that time, energy, and money for nothing.

36

After this experience you'll both probably wish that you had set down your agreement in a written contract. It seems so simple now, with the benefit of hindsight, that you should have entered into a written agreement that clearly spelled out the scope of your services and the fee to be paid. If you had a crystal ball and could know in advance which deals would turn sour, you could feel comfortable setting only those transactions down on paper. But how can you know that? It might help to think of written contracts in the way that fighter pilots view their parachute. They may need that parachute only once in every thousand flights, but they'll be certain to wear it every flight. After all, no one knows which time they'll need that protection.

Make Sure There's a Meeting of the Minds

Clients often believe that they don't need a written contract with so-and-so. "After all," they say, "we're old friends and Jack would never cheat me." What these clients don't realize is that you don't sign a written agreement to prevent someone from cheating you. If you thought someone was dishonest, you wouldn't enter into any business dealings with them. Entering into a written contract with crooks won't ensure you that they will perform their obligations under the contract.

One of the most important reasons to put an agreement in writing is the opportunity it provides both parties to focus on the terms of the transaction. By doing this, you can help to avoid misunderstandings about the underlying business terms. In general, business disputes are not caused by fraud or dishonesty; they are caused by honest misunderstandings between businesspeople. Misunderstandings are much more likely to arise when people have neglected to set down the terms of their agreement in a detailed written document.

If you enter into a business transaction without setting it down on paper, you're more likely to find down the road that you and your colleague didn't share the same understanding of the terms of your transaction, that there wasn't a meeting of the minds. This kind of misunderstanding can have disastrous consequences just as it did in the example of Alpha

Corporation. In Sarah's mind, she had agreed to provide her introductory, one-week TQM seminar to Alpha's senior management. Sarah was hopeful that, as a result of this seminar, senior management would hire her to implement an overall TQM plan throughout the company. Unfortunately, that wasn't the CEO's understanding. He thought that, after this week-long seminar, his senior management would have all the tools necessary to implement their own internal TQM plan, using the written training materials that Sarah had developed.

It's clear that these two businesspeople did not have a meeting of the minds about the scope of the services to be provided. But this does not make either one of them a bad person, and it doesn't mean that either one is dishonest. It just means that there was a basic misunderstanding about the terms of the transaction. That misunderstanding was masked by their failure to put the contract down on paper. In the course of drafting a written contract, their misunderstanding would have become apparent.

If this misunderstanding had surfaced before Sarah provided the services, the two of them could have addressed the issue. One way or another, that misunderstanding would have been resolved. After discussing the problem, they might well have reached agreement on the scope of the services to be provided and on the amount of Sarah's fee for those services. On the other hand, they might have concluded that they just couldn't make a deal. In the latter case, Sarah would have been disappointed but at least she'd have saved herself from the raw deal she eventually got, furnishing services without receiving any fee.

Neither Sarah nor the CEO realized that they were worlds apart on this matter until after Sarah provided the seminar. These two businesspeople ended up in a nasty dispute for one reason only, they didn't put their agreement in writing. They permitted ambiguity and misunderstanding to rule the day. Undoubtedly, if they had negotiated a written agreement, they would have quickly realized that they were talking apples and oranges regarding the scope of services to be provided at the quoted price. Had they sat down to hammer out a written agreement, this basic misunderstanding would have surfaced and they could have addressed the issue up-front. It's true that disputes can arise even when you have a written contract, but it's much more likely for problems to arise when you haven't worked out the terms of the deal beforehand. The most effective and efficient way of doing that is to negotiate and sign a written contract.

Businesspeople often pride themselves on doing business on a hand-shake without getting their lawyers involved. This is somehow supposed to show that they are honorable and can trust each other. But, as you have learned in this chapter, the best way to maintain a good relationship with your business colleagues is to get your agreements down on paper. It's not a question of honor at all. It's simply good business practice. Doing business without written agreements is like playing with matches. It's only a matter of time before you get burned.

Chapter 5

Contractor or Employee

Does It Matter?

Mary had worked for Designer, Inc., a large corporation, as a market research analyst for a number of years. Dissatisfied with her stagnant compensation, Mary had told her boss of her plans to quit. Mary's boss confided to her that his hands were tied regarding her salary because of company policy. However, he suggested to Mary that she quit her job and come back as a full-time consultant to the company. He explained to her that, although she wouldn't be eligible for medical insurance or other employee benefits, he would pay her 30 percent more than she had been earning. Mary took the advice of her boss and became a consultant to the company. For the past year, she has provided consulting services to the company and has been paid significantly more than she received as an employee. Designer, Inc., is her sole client, and the work that she does as a consultant is substantially identical to the work that she was doing for the company as an employee. Mary's boss shared this idea with other managers in the company who made similar arrangements with some of their underpaid employees.

Then one day Mary's boss was abruptly fired from the company. He told her that the IRS had just completed its audit and assessed the company with over $100,000 in employment taxes, penalties, and interest. The IRS concluded that, from a tax standpoint, Mary and all those other consultants were employees of the company rather than independent contractors. Mary's contract was immediately terminated, and she hasn't a clue what happened.

What went wrong for Mary and Designer, Inc.? How did the company end up owing so much in taxes to the IRS for the services they obtained from their consultants? As a consultant, why should you care how the IRS views the services that you provide to your clients?

The Hidden Costs Of Employees

Think back to when you were employed by that big corporation before you entered the world of self-employed consulting. Every time you got a paycheck, there was a big chunk of money taken out by your employer to pay your federal and state income taxes. In addition, your employer took out of your paycheck your FICA (Federal Insurance Contributions Act) taxes to pay your social security and Medicare taxes. These taxes were withheld from your wages and forwarded by your employer on your behalf to the IRS and to your state tax agency.

Payroll Taxes

In addition to withholding income and FICA taxes from its employees' paychecks, an employer is required to pay federal and state payroll taxes out of its own pocket for its employees. A business is required to pay substantial payroll taxes based on the wages it pays to its employees. However, a business is not required to pay these payroll taxes in connection with fees that it pays to its independent contractors. The tax benefits of using independent contractors becomes clear when you consider the scope of these payroll taxes. The payroll taxes that apply to employees of a business are summarized below.

- The employee's share of the FICA taxes must be deducted from the employee's wages and forwarded to the IRS. For social security, the withholding amount is 6.2 percent of the employee's wages up to a current maximum of $68,400, as of 1998. For Medicare, the withholding amount is currently 1.45 percent of the employee's wages, with no maximum limit.
- The employee's federal and state income taxes must be withheld and forwarded to the taxing authority.
- The employer's share of the FICA taxes must be paid by the employer. The employer pays the same amount as the employee for these taxes, currently 6.2 percent of wages up to $68,400 for social security and 1.45 percent of wages for Medicare.
- The employer must pay federal and state unemployment taxes at the applicable tax rates.

These are the payroll taxes required to be paid in connection with an employee's wages. Consider what would happen if that same worker were treated as an independent contractor.

The company is not required to withhold federal and state income taxes for its independent contractors, but this doesn't mean that there's no income tax payable by the worker. Independent contractors is required to report their income on their personal tax return and pay their income taxes directly to the taxing authorities. In addition to income tax, an independent contractor pays a self-employment tax which is equivalent to the combined employer and employee share of the FICA taxes. In other words, an independent contractor pays a self-employment tax equal to 12.4 percent of self-employment income up to $68,400 and 2.9 percent of that income for Medicare tax. So, not surprisingly, the IRS receives the same revenue in personal income and FICA taxes regardless of whether a worker is an independent contractor or an employee, assuming, of course, that independent contractors actually pays their taxes.

In addition, the company is not required to pay the employer's share of the FICA taxes for an independent contractor nor is it required to pay unemployment taxes for that worker. The payroll taxes that a business is required to pay for its employees can mean a substantial add-on to its personnel expense. No wonder it's so tempting to hire independent contractors whenever possible.

Employee Benefits

In addition to paying federal and state payroll taxes based on its employees' wages, businesses incur significant costs for the benefit packages provided to their employees. These can include medical insurance, dental insurance, vacation pay, and retirement programs. With the skyrocketing cost of medical insurance in recent years, the cost of the employee benefit package can be staggering, particularly for small businesses.

Although employees participate in employee benefit programs, independent contractors do not. Using independent contractors instead of employees can therefore result in savings because the company does not incur the expense of the benefit package.

Workers' Compensation

Businesses are also required to obtain workers' compensation insurance for their employees. Workers' compensation is a state-mandated program under which employees receive compensation for work-related injuries. Workers' compensation is a no-fault system, which means that an employee needn't show that their employer was negligent in causing the injury. The trade-off for the employer is that workers' compensation is the exclusive remedy injured workers have against their employers. This means that the employee can't bring suit for negligence and that the employer won't be exposed to a potentially large verdict for pain and suffering and other intangible damages.

The premium for workers' compensation insurance is based on a number of factors including the size of the employer's payroll, the employer's claim history, and the type of services provided by its employees. A moving and storage business, for instance, would have a higher rating for workers' compensation insurance and therefore pay a higher premium per employee than, say, a law firm. In some industries, the cost of obtaining workers' compensation insurance can be substantial.

Under some circumstances, a business that retains an independent contractor can be required to maintain workers compensation insurance for the employees of that independent contractor. For the most part, however, workers' compensation applies to employees but not to independent contractors. This is another reason why using independent contractors can be less expensive for a business than hiring employees.

Employee or Independent Contractor?

It is clear that businesses can benefit financially from hiring independent contractors instead of employees. But recall the story at the beginning of the chapter about Designer, Inc. Even though Designer retained the services of lots of independent contractors, it got into big trouble with the IRS. How could that happen? When it comes to a worker's classification as an employee or an independent contractor, government agencies can examine a company's business practices. The government agency can then reclassify workers and, with a wave of a magic wand, turn independent contractors into employees.

While an IRS audit can result in a reclassification of a company's independent contractors to employees, the IRS isn't the only government agency interested in the classification of workers. A variety of state agencies can reclassify a company's workers. In particular, state labor departments, workers' compensation bureaus, and state taxing authorities can examine businesses to determine if workers are being appropriately treated as independent contractors. Although the general principles are similar, each agency applies its own test in determining a worker's status. So the same worker can be considered an independent contractor for IRS purposes but an employee for workers' compensation purposes.

What do the IRS and other government agencies look at in determining whether a worker is an employee or an independent contractor? In general, if a company has the right to direct and control the way any workers do their job, then those workers are considered to be employees. Conversely, if a company does not have the right to direct and control the way a worker does his or her job other than to accept or reject the final work product, then that worker is considered to be an independent contractor. While a written agreement reflecting the worker's status as an independent contractor is some evidence of status, it is not by any means conclusive. The IRS will look behind the document to see how the transaction is really structured.

The IRS has identified certain factors to help determine a worker's status which are referred to as the 20-factor test. This test is designed to help distinguish between a true employee and an independent contractor. The test includes such factors as:

- Profit and loss. Unlike an employee, an independent contractor can make a profit or suffer a loss on a project.
- Number of clients. Independent contractors usually offer their services to the general public and have more than one client while an employee generally provides services to only one company.
- Set hours of work. An employee usually has set hours of work established by the employer while independent contractors set their own hours.
- Location. Employees usually work on their employer's premises while an independent contractor does not.
- Tools and materials. An employee is usually furnished tools, materials, and other equipment by the employer while independent contractors generally provides their own equipment.

The entire list of 20 factors is given in Appendix C of this book. You should be aware, however, that not all 20 factors are given equal weight. To complicate matters further, the IRS has recently concluded that several of the factors may no longer even be relevant to a worker's status. In a training manual published by the IRS in 1996, both the location and the number of clients, for instance, were deemed to be irrelevant factors in determining a worker's status.

Because this is such an important issue for businesses today, there have been several attempts recently to create objective standards for determining a worker's status. A proposed bill in Congress would have amended the Internal Revenue Code to simplify the IRS determination of independent contractor status, but the bill died a quiet death. A so-called Safe Harbor Rule has recently been adopted under which the IRS is forced to accept the treatment of a worker as an independent contractor if certain requirements are met.

One of these requirements, however, is that the business has a reasonable basis for classifying its workers as independent contractors. Undoubtedly the IRS agent and the businessman will disagree on whether that basis was reasonable, making this a not very safe harbor.

The IRS still has significant discretion in this area and, wherever possible, the IRS will reclassify workers from independent contractors to employees. After all, if businesses only hired employees, think how much easier tax collection would be. Instead of relying on individual independent contractors to pay their own income taxes and self-employment taxes, the IRS could rely on American businesses to be their tax-collection agents.

Misclassification and Its Dire Consequences

If the IRS concludes that a business has misclassified its workers as independent contractors, it can assess substantial tax penalties against the business. At a minimum, the business will be required to pay the employer's share of the worker's FICA taxes. In addition, the business can be required to pay a percentage of the employee's share of the FICA taxes as well as a penalty of up to 20 percent of the worker's wages. These taxes can be assessed against a business even if a worker has already paid all income taxes and FICA taxes required to be paid on that same income. By reclassifying workers as employees, the IRS can end up collecting more taxes than it would otherwise be entitled to. No wonder the IRS agents are so keen on reclassifying workers as employees.

As if IRS penalties weren't bad enough, it can get worse. If the IRS concludes that a business has failed to pay these payroll taxes, it can hold the principals of the business personally liable for those taxes. So even if a business is incorporated, the owners and employees of the corporation can be held personally liable for the company's payroll taxes. Also, if an agency other than the IRS determines that workers have been misclassified and should be treated as employees, the business can face fines and other penalties.

What This Means to You

As a consultant, it's important for you to understand the financial benefits enjoyed by companies that retain your services as an independent contractor. This will help you understand why your services as an independent contractor are so valuable to the company. It can also help you in determining an appropriate fee for your services.

In addition, your clients may ask you what may seem like nosy questions about your business to help verify that you will be treated as an independent contractor. For instance, your client might ask to see a copy of any print advertising you have run or evidence that you maintain business premises. As you have seen, the way you run your consulting business can impact the classification of your status as an independent contractor.

In addition, some businesses will not hire independent contractors who are doing business as sole proprietors, having concluded that the IRS is less likely to challenge the independent contractor status of a business entity. These companies will only hire independent contractors who are corporations or limited liability companies.

Your client will also want to have a written independent contractor agreement with you which not only outlines the business deal but also reflects that the parties intend for you to be an independent contractor and not an employee. Take a look at the sample agreements that are included in Appendix A and Appendix B of this book. And while not binding on the IRS, a written agreement can at least provide evidence of the intent of the parties.

Conversely, you may be in the position of hiring subcontractors to help you with your consulting projects. You too can face the possibility of a misclassification of your workers. Make sure that you don't inadvertently end up with employees instead of independent contractors.

Chapter 6

Written Contracts
When to Use Them and What to Include

No doubt you're now convinced of the importance of using written contracts instead of oral ones. Instead of asking, "When should I bother with a written contract?" you now know that the simple answer is all the time. After all, you never know when you'll need that parachute. However, the detail and complexity of each contract will depend on the specifics of each particular transaction.

Take the example of Frank, who provides consulting services to large manufacturing companies. He called his lawyer shortly before Christmas one year to tell her that a large manufacturer had hired him to implement an in-house training program for all its U.S. and Mexican plants. His fee would be over $100,000. There was only one problem. The manufacturer wanted to pay Frank his entire fee up front before the end of the year — something to do with corporate budgets and internal bookkeeping.

When the lawyer reviewed the very short consulting contract prepared by the corporation, she realized that Frank's biggest protection was not in the words on the page but in the fact that he was being paid his entire fee up front. Of course it was still important to make sure that the contract accurately described the scope of the services to be provided and that it covered other standard contract provisions. But Frank didn't need to be concerned about such issues as payment terms or remedies in the event of a breach by the client. He would have his money in hand and could take immense comfort in that. A short contract could well do the job he needed. But, mind you, if the lawyer had represented the manufacturing company, that contract would have been a mile long. After all, the manufacturer was most at risk in that situation by paying the entire consulting fee before any services had been provided.

You need to enter into a written contract with each and every one of your consulting clients. Whether you're in the business of developing software, implementing training programs, preparing business plans, or anything else, the success of your business is solely dependent on the fees you earn from your clients. The more you can do to ensure your clients' satisfaction, the more successful your business will be. Doing what you can to avoid disputes with your clients makes good, solid business sense. Making sure that you and your clients are really in agreement about your job will go a long way to ensuring good client relations. There's no question that written contracts are a valuable way to accomplish this.

Next you'll look at the important areas to address in your contracts with your clients. In addition, a sample consulting agreement and a sample subcontractor agreement are included in the appendices of this book.

Parties to the Contract

There will generally be only two parties to your consulting contracts, you and the other person. Remember that, if you have formed an entity of limited liability, you are not really a party to this contract at all. Your entity is the contracting party. Make sure that all of your contracts are entered into by your business entity and not by you personally. Otherwise, you will not benefit from that important protection from personal liability.

The consulting contract needs to identify that the entity, the corporation or the LLC, will be providing the services. If appropriate, you can identify within the contract that you, or some other named individual, will be the person designated by the entity to furnish the contracted services. Your client may feel more comfortable if the contract identifies the specific individuals who will be providing the services. This can be particularly important in a personal service business.

Don't forget that you are signing the contract on behalf of the entity and not personally. If you have formed a corporation, then you are signing contracts as an officer of that corporation, probably as its president. If you have formed a limited liability company, then you are signing contracts as an agent of the LLC, either as a manager if the LLC is manager-operated or as a member of the LLC. Unless you execute contracts on behalf of the entity, you are exposing yourself to personal liability for those contractual obligations. The signature block in your contracts should look something like this:

XYZ Corporation   or   XYZ Limited Liability Company

By _____   By _____

Its President   Its Manager (or Member)

Now look at the other side of this equation. Who are you contracting with? Is it an individual, a corporation, or any other kind of business entity? If your client is a corporation or an LLC, are you comfortable that the business has sufficient assets to pay your fee? If not, you should consider obtaining the personal guarantee of one or more of the principals of the business. Then keep in mind that you too may be asked to personally guarantee your entity's contracts.

Scope of Services

The description of the goods or services that you will be providing is one of the most important parts of your consulting contract. As you have seen, unless you clearly identify the goods or services that you are providing, you can wind up in a mine field of misunderstandings and, quite possibly, in litigation.

Be sure to list exactly what services you will be providing and what products, if any, you are furnishing. If, for example, you are contracting to install a computer network for a client with ten stand-alone computer terminals, you need to identify the exact type of network you will be installing and whether or not the fee includes the cost of any parts that may be required.

It's also important to identify the delivery or completion date. If the contract provides that time is of the essence, then any deadlines in the contract must be strictly complied with. Otherwise, under general contract law, the parties usually are afforded a so-called reasonable time within which to perform their obligations.

Compensation

Your consulting contracts need to describe in detail the compensation that you will be paid for your work. How much will you be paid? Is it a flat fee or is it on a time basis of hourly, daily, or otherwise? Will you be paid weekly, monthly, or at completion? Do you require clients to furnish a retainer prior to your starting work? If so, is the retainer applied against the first bill, the last bill, or otherwise? Are you entitled to reimbursement of any expenses? It's important that you nail down not only the amount of your fee but also all the details of how and when it will be paid.

Copyright

Copyright law protects original works of authorship including books, manuals, reports, films, photographs, graphic designs, computer software, plans, and blueprints. When you have created an original piece of work, you are the owner of the copyright on that work. As the owner of the copyright, you have certain exclusive rights, including the right to copy and distribute that work and to prepare derivative products based on that work. You also have the right to assign, license, or otherwise transfer all or any part of your rights as copyright owner of that work.

In addition to providing expertise in your specific field, you may be delivering to your clients a tangible work product as part of your services. That work product may be a software program, manual, report, or any other tangible product that you deliver to your client as part of your consulting services.

Assume that you are a management training consultant and have been retained to provide a customized management-training manual for your client. The scope of your client's rights to use that manual is very important to your client and to you. You may expect that the client will use that manual for a limited purpose such as internal training. But can your client display the manual on its web page? Can it sell the manual to other companies in the field without paying you additional compensation? Are you limited in your use of boiler-plate portions of the training manual when you prepare customized training manuals for other clients? The answers to these questions depend on what your consulting contract specifies.

Your client may ask you to assign to them all rights in the work product that you are delivering as part of your consulting services. Whether it makes sense for you to sign over all of your rights will depend on the specifics of your situation. By all means, though, you will want to explore the alternatives.

One option is to grant to your client a perpetual non-exclusive license to use the work product within the company at no additional charge. That gives your client the right to use the work product, and because it's a non-exclusive license, it doesn't limit your right to use your work product for other clients. Be very careful that you don't inadvertently assign to your client exclusive rights to valuable materials that you will need for future jobs.

Similar copyright issues exist between you and your subcontractors. If you have agreed to assign all rights to a software program or written report to your client, make sure that any of your subcontractors who contribute to that work assign to you all of their rights in the project.

Without these assignments, you will not be able to live up to your agreement with your client.

As you can see, copyright issues can be very complex. Your best bet is to speak with an experienced copyright attorney to obtain advice specific to your needs.

Confidentiality and Non-solicitation

If you will be provided access to your client's database or other confidential information in the course of providing your consulting services, you will probably be asked to abide by a confidentiality agreement. This protects the client from your using or disclosing any confidential information that you obtain in the course of providing your services. This is a standard practice in many industries such as software consulting.

The scope of the confidentiality agreement, however, should be closely reviewed. If you do agree to a confidentiality provision, make sure that you obtain similar confidentiality agreements from anyone that you hire to help you on the project, whether they are your employees or independent contractors.

You may be revealing certain confidential information to your client about your own know-how, such as technology, techniques, or business methods, in the course of providing your consulting services. If so, you ought to get a confidentiality agreement from the client to protect your proprietary secrets.

Your client may seek to prohibit you from soliciting any of its personnel for your own employment. If your client is bringing you on board for a particular consulting project, they don't want you to use it as an opportunity to raid their experienced personnel. Don't be surprised if you're asked to refrain from this kind of solicitation. But you needn't agree to an open-ended provision. A one-year solicitation prohibition should be more than adequate. You may also want your client to agree that they won't solicit any of your personnel for a similar period of time.

Guarantees

If you are providing any guarantees to your clients regarding the service or product that you are furnishing, make sure this is reflected in your contracts. Also, if you are not providing any guarantee, this needs to be clearly stated in your contracts. Consider this example.

Joe is an efficiency consultant for heavy manufacturers. After examining the manufacturing methods used by his clients, Joe makes recommendations designed to save the client money in their manufacturing process. Joe summarizes his findings and makes recommendations in a written report provided to the manufacturer. The report describes potential savings that the manufacturer can achieve by implementing the proposals.

Assume that one of Joe's clients implements Joe's plan. Two months later, Joe gets a call from the client claiming that they are not saving money at all, and in fact, their production costs have gone up by 25 percent. The client says that they are reversing all the changes that Joe recommended and that they expect a full refund of Joe's consulting fee as well as payment of $100,000 for the additional manufacturing costs incurred.

Joe's client claims that Joe guaranteed the savings shown in his report. Joe responds that he makes recommendations based on his professional opinion but that he doesn't guarantee any specific results. Joe then points to the provision in their signed written contract that states: "Consultant makes no representations, warranties, or guarantees regarding the actual savings, if any, that client will achieve by implementing the recommendations made by consultant."

Now Joe is a sensible businessman and does what he can to satisfy this dissatisfied client, but there's no more talk of paying $100,000 in damages.

And you thought all these stories had bad endings. It just goes to show you how valuable those written contracts can be.

Additional Contract Provisions

In addition to the contract provisions that are specific to your consulting business, your contracts with your clients should contain provisions more generally applicable to all commercial contracts. These include:

- Termination of the contract. Can one or both parties terminate the contract? If so, what period of notice is required and is there a termination fee payable?
- Remedies for breach of contract. This includes the right to collect attorneys' fees in the event of a dispute.
- Governing law. This will vary by state.

Get Subcontractor Agreements in Writing

You will undoubtedly be relying on the services of subcontractors in your consulting business from time to time. Perhaps you're a public relations consultant retained to create and produce a promotional brochure for your client. While you will be the mastermind of the project, you will also need to rely on other professionals to help you produce the finished product. Perhaps you'll need the services of a photographer, a graphic designer, a copywriter, a printer. Each one of those people is a subcontractor to you, and each one of them is crucial to the success of your project and to your ability to satisfy your client.

If you've committed to delivery of the finished product by December 1, you'll need a final proof of the brochure no later than November 1. If the graphic designers are under the impression that they can deliver on their part of the project in mid-November, where will that leave you? Clearly, you'll be scrambling around in early November trying desperately to fix this oversight.

For the same reasons that you need written contracts with your clients, you also need written contracts with your subcontractors. You certainly don't want any misunderstanding about the services your subcontractor will provide to you or the delivery deadlines, nor do you want any disputes about the fee that you owe your subcontractors. If you've priced the project according to the fees quoted to you by your subcontractors, you don't want to be faced with a demand for greater fees. That could leave you with no profit left in the job for you.

During a legal workshop for consultants, one of the participants shared her own experience with a subcontractor. Jane is an event organizer. She had recently organized a conference for the Small Business Administration. Part of Jane's job as the conference organizer was to arrange for a photographer to take pictures throughout the day at the conference.

About two weeks before the conference, the photographer called Jane to say that his fee would be 25 percent higher than he had originally quoted her. Jane was annoyed with the photographer's attempt to squeeze her for more money. However, she was relieved that she had a written contract with the photographer detailing exactly what services he would provide and the fee to be paid.

When she reminded the photographer of the terms of their written contract, he soon backed down. The photographer came to the conference and performed his services in accordance with the terms of that contract.

The two contracts, the consulting contract with your client and the subcontract agreement with your subcontractor, present similar issues. In the first instance, you are providing specified goods or services for which you will receive an agreed-upon fee. In the second, you are receiving specified goods or services for which you will pay an agreed-upon fee.

For the most part, the two contracts will be similar. But you are wearing a different hat in each of these contracts. You may, for instance, include a strict deadline in your subcontractor agreements so that you'll be able to deliver to your client on time. On the other hand, you may give yourself more leeway in your delivery time to your consulting clients.

Form Contracts

In this chapter, you have reviewed the kinds of provisions that you need to include in your written contracts. To be prepared, you may want to have your attorney prepare at least two standard form contracts for you, one to use with your consulting clients and another to use with your subcontractors. The contract can leave blanks for you to fill in for each particular transaction, or it can refer to an addendum which you can complete and attach to the contract.

If an unusual issue arises, however, or if you find yourself negotiating the legal parts of the contract, it's best to consult with your attorney.

Chapter 7

A Good Business Lawyer
How to Choose One and How to Use One

Whether you're starting a new business or operating an existing business, you will need to address a variety of legal issues. Perhaps you're planning to form an entity of limited liability or enter into a lease of business premises. Maybe you're taking out a business loan or obtaining financing from friends or relatives. No doubt you'll be negotiating business contracts with clients, suppliers, employees, and independent contractors, to name but a few.

If you're operating your business out of your home, you may be concerned about compliance with local zoning restrictions. These are just a few of the legal matters you may need to address in operating your business.

How to Choose a Good Business Lawyer

Clearly what's required is a good business attorney to help you address the legal needs of your business. There are a number of ways to find a business attorney. You can ask your colleagues if they know of a good business lawyer. You can also ask your accountant to recommend some-one. You might check with the small business resource organizations in your community, such as the Service Corps of Retired Executives (SCORE), the Small Business Administration, or the Small Business Development Center. You can also call the Small Business Admin-istration's toll-free number listed in Appendix D.

After you've collected the names of a few business lawyers, you'll need to chose the one that's right for you. Lawyers will often provide an ini-tial consultation at no charge. This allows both you and the lawyer to meet and get to know each other. The lawyer will probably ask you about your business and what legal services you think you need. You can ask the lawyer about his or her experience representing small businesses like yours. Why not ask what kind of business entity he or she would rec-ommend for your business and what it would cost to form the entity. Find out about legal fees. Is it on an hourly basis? What is the billing rate? Does the lawyer offer a fixed-fee alternative?

You should meet with a few lawyers so that you can compare them. In evaluating a lawyer, some of the areas to look at are:

- Competence. Your lawyer should be experienced in representing small businesses. A lawyer who is great at handling house closings or litigation may not know much about business law.

- Communication skills. Communication is a two-way street. Your lawyer should be able to listen to you and understand your concerns. In addition, you need to be able to understand the information and advice your lawyer gives you. Your lawyer needs to explain your legal rights and obligations in a comprehensible manner to help you make appropriate decisions. Otherwise, how can you feel comfortable rely-ing on your lawyers' recommendations?

- Responsiveness. Whether the lawyer responds to your legal needs in a timely manner, returns your phone calls quickly, and delivers on schedule are all good indications of how the lawyer values you as a client.

- Fees. Legal fees are an important factor but not the only factor in choosing a lawyer. It is essential that you and your lawyer agree up-front about the fee arrangement. Realize that it's like any other pur-chase and that cheapest isn't necessarily best.

- Style. Lawyers have different styles, the same as other people. Make sure that your lawyer's style is right for you. Otherwise, you won't be able to develop a comfortable, trusting relationship. To assess a lawyer's style, ask yourself these questions: Do they have a relaxed manner or is it too formal? Do they lecture you about the law or put it in terms that you can easily understand? Do they make the time to answer your questions?

Whether you are hiring your first business lawyer or are thinking of changing lawyers, these considerations will help you make the best choice.

How to Use Your Business Lawyer

Particularly in the early days of operating your business, you're likely to have numerous legal questions. Even something as apparently simple as opening a business bank account can raise legal questions. When you see some of those bank forms, you'll know why even very experienced corporate paralegals can end up chewing their fingernails over the bank account authorization forms.

If you have a legal question or problem, you should by all means feel comfortable calling your lawyer. If it's something simple, chances are they'll be able to answer it right away and probably not charge you for the call. If it's more complex, find out what will be involved in getting an answer and how much it will cost you.

You should seek the advice of your business lawyer whenever you have a legal question or concern. Some of the important ways in which your business lawyer can help you are regarding:

- Preparation of standard form contracts. If there are contracts that you use on a regular basis, ask your lawyer to provide you with a standard form contract tailored for your use. These include consulting agreements, independent contractor agreements, and employment agreements. But remember that it is only a form and you'll need to consult with your lawyer if there is any unusual aspect of the transaction that may need to be specifically addressed.

- Assistance in negotiating contracts. You may run into difficulties in negotiating the terms of a transaction. Perhaps your potential landlord is requiring you to personally guarantee the lease, and you are unwilling to do so. There may be a middle ground that both parties can live with, such as a guarantee of a limited dollar amount or of a limited duration. A good business lawyer can help you devise creative solutions in areas of disagreement. Lawyers can use their extensive experience in similar business transactions to help you to achieve a win-win result.

- Leasing business premises. Make sure you have your lawyer review any lease before you sign it. That way your lawyer can check whether the agreement reflects your understanding of the business deal. Also, your lawyer can make suggestions to protect your interests under the lease.

- Financing. If you're taking out a bank loan or getting any other type of financing, you'll want your lawyer's assistance. While you are focused on the cash requirements of your business, your lawyer can help structure the transaction to protect your interests.

- Intellectual property. If you are creating materials such as software programs as part of your business, you will want to protect your property rights in those assets. This may require registering them for copyright protection with the federal Patent and Trademark Office. You will definitely need an experienced lawyer to help with this process. Patent and trademark law are specialized areas of legal practice. Your business lawyer can probably recommend a good patent and trademark lawyer to help you.

Handling Your Own Legal Matters

There is an old adage that says, "The lawyer who represents himself has a fool for a client." The same can be said, for different reasons, about the non-lawyer representing himself. There are so many self-help legal books on the market these days that you may be thinking about handling your own legal matters without an attorney. "Form Your Own

Corporation" touts one book. "Small Business Legal Forms — Save on Unnecessary Legal Fees" claims another. You can certainly save money in the short term handling your own legal matters, but what about the long-term costs?

Your lawyer can help you structure and document your business transactions to protect your interests. If you're having difficulty negotiating a business transaction, your lawyer can help by offering creative solutions that address both parties' concerns. If you do end up in a business dispute, your lawyer can help you to analyze the merits and weaknesses of your position. You can then make an informed decision about settling the dispute. If you don't end up settling, then it's your lawyer who will champion your cause through the judicial system. These are just a few of the areas in which your lawyer's help can be invaluable.

If you have a legal problem, should you handle it yourself or should you get help from an expert? If your microwave oven wasn't working, how would you fix that? You could go to the library and read every book on electronics and then read every repair book for kitchen equipment. After you'd finished your studies, you could tackle that oven. But what's the likelihood you'd be able to fix it yourself even then? A call to an experienced repairperson, on the other hand, would be quicker, more efficient, and possibly less expensive than trying to do it yourself. Because of their training and wealth of experience with similar problems, a repairperson should be able to spot the problem and repair the oven quickly. Or, after spotting the problem, the repairperson may advise you that it's not worth repairing it because it would be cheaper to buy a new one. Isn't it more sensible to rely on the expert than to try and learn about every field yourself?

Handling your own legal matters is a lot like trying to fix your microwave oven. Sure, it's possible to read enough on the subject and talk to enough other amateurs to be able to handle a simple legal problem for yourself. But, surely, life's too short for that. There must be more productive ways for you to spend your time in building up your consulting business than pouring over dusty law books. An experienced business lawyer can help you resolve your legal problems smoothly and efficiently.

This is not to say that you need never do any research into legal matters. Clients should have a general understanding of their legal rights and obligations. By all means, read as many books and articles and leaflets about law as you want. This will help you to better understand your legal rights and obligations. It will also make it easier for you and your lawyer to communicate. You'll be able to ask the right questions and to understand your lawyer's advice more easily. It might even give you a better appreciation for what your lawyer is doing for you.

Conclusion

According to Gale's *Consultants and Consulting Organizations Directory*, which currently lists over 20,000 consulting firms in the U.S. and Canada, consulting is a healthy, growing, and dynamic segment of the economy. The variety of consulting fields is growing constantly. The traditional fields of consulting such as business consultants, management consultants, and computer consultants are being joined by consultants in every field imaginable. These include bridal consultants, agricultural consultants, roofing consultants, image consultants, church management consultants, marine consultants, theater consultants, and publishing consultants to name a few. Each of these even has its own trade association.

Tremendous opportunities exist today for consultants with marketable skills. The sky's the limit. Don't be frightened by the doomsayers amongst us. Sure there are risks of going into business for yourself. There are risks associated with anything you do, even crossing the street. The key is to arm yourself with knowledge. That way you can follow your course with confidence in your actions. This book is meant to help you on your journey into the exciting world of consulting.

Consulting Agreement

By using a written consulting agreement for each and every one of your consulting projects, you can help to ensure that you and your client are really in agreement about the terms of the transaction. It's important to clearly define the scope of your services as well as the compensation arrangement. Other issues such as delivery dates and copyright ownership are also important.

This sample consulting agreement will alert you to the kinds of issues that need to be covered in your agreements. However, it is always important to obtain the advice of an experienced attorney to help you prepare an agreement that suits your particular needs.

Consulting Agreement

This AGREEMENT is entered into by and between SMITH MANUFACTURING EFFICIENCY CONSULTING LLC, a Connecticut limited liability company ("Consultant") and CLIENT CORPORATION, a Connecticut corporation ("Client").

> *Comment:* If you have formed a corporation or limited liability company for your consulting business, remember that it is the entity and not you personally that is a party to the agreement.

STATEMENT OF FACTS

A. Consultant is engaged in the business of providing manufacturing efficiency services; and

B. Client seeks to engage Consultant to provide manufacturing efficiency services at its Middletown factory as provided herein.

> *Comment:* Although this consultant is providing manufacturing efficiency services, the provisions in this contract are relevant to consultants in general.

NOW, THEREFORE, for good and valuable consideration the receipt and sufficiency of which are hereby acknowledged, the parties enter into this Agreement.

> *Comment:* A recital of consideration is standard in any contract because a lack of consideration can result in a contract being unenforceable.

1. Services. Consultant is hereby engaged to provide to Client those manufacturing efficiency services at its Middletown factory specified in the attached Addendum A (the "Services"). Client acknowledges that Consultant may engage one or more subcontractors to assist Consultant in rendering the Services hereunder. Consultant, its employees, agents, and subcontractors shall have access to Client's premises and property during normal working hours for the purpose of performing the Services.

> *Comment:* The services to be provided need to be spelled out in detail in the addendum to the agreement. If there is a misunderstanding about the scope of your services, there is sure to be trouble down the road.

2. Compensation. Client shall pay compensation to Consultant for the Services to be provided hereunder at the per diem rate of $_____ per (eight-hour) work day.

To the extent that the Services are provided in time-blocks other than eight-hour work days, compensation shall be paid at the rate of $_____ per hour. Consultant shall submit a detailed invoice to Client on a bi-weekly basis, which invoices shall be due and payable within ten days after the invoice date.

Except for reimbursable expenses as provided herein, Consultant shall be responsible for all of its own costs and expenses, including without limitation, overhead expenses, equipment, materials, rent, telephones, and electricity. Client shall reimburse Consultant only for such specific out-of-pocket expenses incurred by Consultant in the discharge of its obligations under this Agreement as have been previously approved by Client.

> *Comment:* The contract must specify the compensation you will receive for your services. If payment will be on a time basis, specify the rates to be paid. If payment will be on a project basis, specify the benchmarks to be achieved for installment payments.

3. Term. The initial term of this Agreement shall commence on _____ and shall continue for a period of _____ thereafter. Either party may, however, terminate this Agreement at any time by furnishing the other party ten days' written notice of termination. Notwithstanding termination of this Agreement, however, those provisions which provide for a longer effective period, such as the confidentiality provisions, shall remain in full force and effect as provided therein.

> *Comment:* The specifics of the termination provision, like everything else in the contract, are subject to negotiation between you and your client. You may want a fixed-term contract of six months or a year, or you may both be agreeable to a mutual right to terminate with a prescribed notice period. As a general rule, the termination provisions of the contract should be even-handed, meaning that what's good for one party should be good for the other.

4. Confidentiality. Consultant agrees to maintain as confidential all Confidential Information (as hereinafter defined) made available to Consultant by Client in connection with the rendering of Services hereunder. All Confidential Information shall be maintained as confidential with the exception of such disclosure as Client may consent to in writing. Confidential Information shall mean information furnished by Client of a confidential nature which is identified in writing to be confidential, or if disclosed orally, is specified and confirmed in writing to be confidential within 30 days after such oral disclosure. Confidential Information does not

include information which is: (a) known to Consultant prior to disclosure by Client; (b) in the public domain through no wrongful act of Consultant; or (c) independently acquired by Consultant from a third party with the right to disclose such information. Consultant shall use substantially similar means to protect the Confidential Information as Consultant uses in protecting its own trade secrets and proprietary information. Prior to disclosure of Confidential Information to any of its employees or other authorized persons, Consultant shall obtain an appropriate signed confidentiality agreement from all such persons. Upon termination of this Agreement, Consultant shall deliver and turn over to Client any and all Confidential Information which has come into its possession. This confidentiality requirement shall expire three years from the date hereof.

> *Comment:* Your client will be concerned about disclosing confidential information about its business operations to an outsider such as yourself. It is reasonable for the client to require you to maintain the confidentiality of its trade secrets and other confidential information. The client may request a very broad confidentiality agreement, but you will need to look closely at the provisions. For instance, is everything you learn or observe while on the consulting job to be considered confidential? In this sample agreement, the client must identify in writing those materials which it considers confidential. It may be appropriate, as was done here, to include a time frame in the confidentiality provision rather than to require an open-ended obligation. After all, just about all information becomes stale after a period of time. For an excellent discussion of confidentiality agreements, as well as consulting agreements, see *Write Your Own Business Contracts* by Attorney E. Thorpe Barrett, published by The Oasis Press.

5. Relationship. The parties acknowledge that Consultant shall perform the Services hereunder as an independent contractor and nothing contained herein shall be deemed to create any joint venture, partnership, or agency or employee relationship between the parties hereto, nor shall either party have the right, power, or authority, whether express or implied, to incur any liability on behalf of the other party. The parties further acknowledge that Client will have no obligation whatsoever to provide any employee benefits or privileges of any kind or nature to Consultant, including, without limitation, insurance benefits or pension benefits. Further, Consultant acknowledges that Client is not responsible to collect or withhold federal, state, or local taxes, including income taxes and social security taxes, and that any and all such taxes imposed as a result of this Agreement shall be paid by Consultant.

Comment: See Chapter 5 for a detailed explanation of why your client will want to make sure that you will be considered an independent contractor by the IRS and other government agencies.

6. Sales Tax. Client shall be liable for payment of any sales tax that may be imposed as a result of the Services rendered hereunder. Any such tax shall be in addition to the compensation payable to Consultant hereunder.

   Comment: See Chapter 3 for a discussion of sales tax on consulting services.

7. Remedies. No express or implied warranty is furnished in connection with the Services to be furnished hereunder. Neither party shall be liable to the other or to any third party for any indirect, incidental, special, or consequential damages whether based on contract, tort, or any other legal theory.

   Comment: Remember the example in Chapter 6 about the efficiency expert whose client was dissatisfied with the purported costs savings noted in the consultant's report? Unless you intend to guarantee certain results, you will want to include a disclaimer such as this.

8. Ownership of Work Product. Consultant shall retain any and all rights Consultant may have in any reports or other materials prepared in connection with the Services hereunder (the "Work Product"). Subject to full payment of all sums due hereunder, Consultant hereby grants Client an unrestricted, non-exclusive, perpetual, fully paid-up, worldwide license to use the Work Product within Client's business.

   Comment: The ownership of property rights for the materials that you furnish to your client is a very important issue. Clients often seek an assignment of all rights in the work product. If you agree to this, you will need to make sure that any subcontractors or other third parties who are contributing to the work product have assigned all of their rights in the work product to you. Also, be careful not to inadvertently assign background technology or expertise which you will need to use on consulting jobs for other clients.

9. Notice. Any notice to be provided hereunder shall be delivered by certified mail, return receipt requested, or by reputable overnight courier to the following addresses:

_____   _____

_____   _____

_____   _____

_____   _____

_____   _____

10. Agreement. This Agreement contains the complete agreement of the parties and supersedes any other agreements, written or oral, between the parties.

11. Severability. If any provision of this Agreement shall be held to be invalid or unenforceable for any reason, the remaining provisions shall continue to be valid and enforceable.

12. Non-waiver. The failure of either party to enforce any provision of this Agreement shall not be construed as a waiver or limitation of that party's right to subsequently enforce and compel strict compliance with every provision of this Agreement.

13. Applicable Law. This Agreement shall be governed by the laws of the State of Connecticut.

14. Binding. This Agreement shall be binding upon, and inure to the benefit of, the parties and their respective heirs, successors, and assigns.

Dated as of _____.

SMITH MANUFACTURING
EFFICIENCY CONSULTING LLC   CLIENT CORPORATION

By _____   By _____
Its Manager   Its

Subcontractor Agreement

This sample subcontractor agreement has been drafted for use by the hypothetical manufacturing efficiency consultant who will be hiring Mary Brown as a subcontractor to assist with the project for the client corporation. As with any form agreement, it is important to obtain the advice of an experienced attorney to help you prepare an agreement that suits your particular needs.

Subcontractor Agreement

This AGREEMENT is entered into by and between SMITH MANUFACTURING EFFICIENCY CONSULTING LLC, a Connecticut limited liability company ("Consultant") and MARY BROWN ("Subcontractor").

> *Comment:* Remember that, if you have formed a corporation or limited liability company for your consulting business, it is the entity and not you personally that is a party to the agreement.

STATEMENT OF FACTS

A. Consultant is engaged in the business of providing manufacturing efficiency services;

B. Subcontractor has expertise, knowledge, and skills in the field of manufacturing efficiency; and

C. Consultant seeks to engage Subcontractor to assist in providing manufacturing efficiency services for a specific project which Consultant has contracted to perform for Client Corporation at its Middletown factory all as provided herein.

NOW, THEREFORE, for good and valuable consideration the receipt and sufficiency of which are hereby acknowledged, the parties enter into this Agreement.

> *Comment:* A recital of consideration is standard in any contract because a lack of consideration can result in a contract being unenforceable.

1. Services. Subcontractor is hereby engaged to perform the services specified in the attached Addendum A (the "Services") in connection with the manufacturing efficiency project that Consultant has contracted to perform for Client Corporation (the "Client") at its Middletown factory. The Services shall be performed at Client's place of business, or at Consultant's place of business, as appropriate from time to time.

> *Comment:* For the same reasons that the scope of services in your consulting contracts needs to be clearly spelled out, you also need your subcontractor's services to be clear and complete.

2. Compensation. Consultant shall pay compensation to Subcontractor for the Services to be provided hereunder at the per diem rate of $_____ per (eight-hour)

work day. To the extent that the Services are provided in time-blocks other than eight-hour work days, compensation shall be paid at the rate of $_____ per hour. Subcontractor shall submit a detailed invoice to Consultant on a bi-weekly basis stating the number of hours worked during such period, together with a summary of the services performed. Such invoices shall be due and payable within 15 days after receipt of the invoice.

Except for reimbursable expenses as provided herein, Subcontractor shall be responsible for all of her own costs and expenses, including without limitation, overhead expenses, equipment, materials, rent, telephones, and electricity. Consultant shall reimburse Subcontractor only for such specific out-of-pocket expenses incurred by Subcontractor in the discharge of her obligations under this Agreement as have been previously approved by Consultant.

> *Comment:* You want to avoid any misunderstanding about the fee you will be paying your subcontractor. Also, you want to make sure that your fee schedule with your subcontractor dovetails with the schedule of payments from your client. In these sample contracts, the client is required to pay within ten days after invoice date and the consultant is required to pay the subcontractor within 15 days after the subcontractor presents her invoice. Be very conscious of this timing so you're not squeezed for payments to your subcontractors.

3. Term. The initial term of this Agreement shall commence on _____ and shall continue for a period of _____ thereafter. Consultant may terminate this Agreement at any time, however, without prior notice, if Client terminates its Contract with Consultant for any reason. Notwithstanding termination of this Agreement, however, those provisions which provide for a longer effective period, such as the confidentiality provisions, shall remain in full force and effect as provided therein.

> *Comment:* You will want to make sure that the termination provisions in your subcontractor agreement are consistent with the termination provisions in your consulting contract. If your consulting contract is terminable by either party on 30 days' notice but your subcontractor agreement obligates you to pay for a fixed term, you could be in trouble.

4. Confidentiality. Subcontractor agrees to maintain as confidential any confidential, non-public information or trade secrets regarding Client's business obtained by Subcontractor in connection with the rendering of Services hereunder. All such

information shall be maintained as confidential with the exception of such disclosure as Client and Consultant may consent to in writing. Subcontractor further agrees to maintain as confidential any confidential, non-public information or trade secrets of Consultant regarding Consultant's business including, without limitation, Consultant's client list. Confidential information does not include information which is: (a) known to Subcontractor prior to disclosure by Client or Consultant; (b) in the public domain through no wrongful act of Subcontractor; or (c) independently acquired by Subcontractor from a third party with the right to disclose such information. Upon termination of this Agreement, Subcontractor shall deliver and turn over to Consultant any and all confidential information which has come into her possession.

> *Comment:* This consultant has agreed to a confidentiality provision in its consulting agreement with its client. The consultant must therefore be sure to obtain appropriate confidentiality agreements from its subcontractors who will be privy to the client's confidential information. In this sample subcontractor agreement, the confidentiality requirement is quite broad. The subcontractor is also required to maintain as confidential any confidential information regarding the consultant's business. In certain instances, consultants go even further by requiring that the subcontractor not undertake work directly for the same client for a specified period of time.

5. Relationship. The parties acknowledge that Subcontractor shall perform the Services hereunder as an independent contractor, and nothing contained herein shall be deemed to create any joint venture, partnership, or agency or employee relationship between the parties hereto, nor shall either party have the right, power, or authority, whether express or implied, to incur any liability on behalf of the other party. The parties further acknowledge that Consultant will have no obligation whatsoever to provide any employee benefits or privileges of any kind or nature to Subcontractor, including, without limitation, insurance benefits or pension benefits. Further, Subcontractor acknowledges that Consultant is not responsible to collect or withhold federal, state, or local taxes, including income taxes and social security taxes, and that any and all such taxes imposed as a result of this Agreement shall be paid by Subcontractor.

> *Comment:* See Chapter 5 for a detailed explanation of why you want to make sure that your subcontractors will be considered independent contractors by the IRS and other government agencies.

6. Ownership of Work Product. Subcontractor hereby assigns to Consultant all right, title, and interest in any and all creations, discoveries, inventions, reports, drawings, designs, software, blueprints, data, writings and technical information, and any other creative achievements made, prepared, or developed by Subcontractor in the course of furnishing Services hereunder, whether alone or with others, and whether or not the same or any part thereof is capable of being patented, trade-marked, copyrighted, or otherwise protected. Subcontractor shall assist Consultant on request during and following the termination of this Agreement, at Consultant's expense, to obtain and maintain for Consultant's own benefit, patent and/or copyright registration for any such inventions and or copyrightable work in any and all countries.

> *Comment:* This is a very broad assignment of rights for the work product contributed to this project by the subcontractor. In fact, it is much broader than the comparable provision in the sample consulting agreement.

7. Indemnity. Contractor shall indemnify, save, and hold Consultant harmless from any claims, actions, damages, judgments, costs, or expenses, including attorneys' fees, arising out of the acts or omissions of Subcontractor in connection with the Services to be rendered hereunder.

> *Comment:* If your subcontractor screws up on your project, you can be held liable to your client for any damages. If that were to happen, you would want the right to recover against your subcontractor. You may also want confirmation that your subcontractor is maintaining adequate liability insurance to cover such a risk.

8. Notice. Any notice to be provided hereunder shall be delivered by certified mail, return receipt requested, or by reputable overnight courier to the following addresses:

_____   _____

_____   _____

_____   _____

_____   _____

9. Agreement. This Agreement contains the complete agreement of the parties and supersedes any other agreements, written or oral, between the parties.

10. Severability. If any provision of this Agreement shall be held to be invalid or unenforceable for any reason, the remaining provisions shall continue to be valid and enforceable.

11. Non-waiver. The failure of either party to enforce any provision of this Agreement shall not be construed as a waiver or limitation of that party's right to subsequently enforce and compel strict compliance with every provision of this Agreement.

12. Applicable Law. This Agreement shall be governed by the laws of the State of Connecticut.

13. Binding. This Agreement shall be binding upon, and inure to the benefit of, the parties and their respective heirs, successors and assigns.

Dated as of _____.

SMITH MANUFACTURING
EFFICIENCY CONSULTING LLC

By _____   _____
Its Manager   Mary Brown

IRS Common-law Rules

To help you determine whether an individual is an employee under the common-law rules, the IRS has identified 20 factors that are used as guidelines to determine whether sufficient control is present to establish an employer and employee relationship.

These factors should be considered guidelines. Not every factor is applicable in every situation, and the degree of importance of each factor varies depending on the type of work and individual circumstances. However, all relevant factors are considered in making a determination, and no one factor is decisive.

It does not matter that a written agreement may take a position with regard to any factors or state that certain factors do not apply, if the facts indicate otherwise. If an employer treats an employee as an independent contractor and certain relief provisions do not apply, the person responsible for the collection and payment of withholding taxes may be held personally liable for an amount equal to the taxes that should have been withheld.

The 20 factors indicating whether an individual is an employee or an independent contractor follow.

1. Instructions. An employee must comply with instructions about when, where, and how to work. Even if no instructions are given, the control factor is present if the employer has the right to control how the work results are achieved.

2. Training. An employee may be trained to perform services in a particular manner. Independent contractors ordinarily use their own methods and receive no training from the purchasers of their services.

3. Integration. An employee's services are usually integrated into the business operations because the services are important to the success or continuation of the business. This shows that the employee is subject to direction and control.

4. Services rendered personally. An employee renders services personally. This shows that the employer is interested in the methods as well as the results.

5. Hiring assistants. An employee works for an employer who hires, supervises, and pays workers. An independent contractor can hire, supervise, and pay assistants under a contract that requires him or her to provide materials and labor and to be responsible only for the result.

6. Continuing relationship. An employee generally has a continuing relationship with an employer. A continuing relationship may exist even if work is performed at recurring although irregular intervals.

7. Set hours of work. An employee usually has set hours of work established by an employer. An independent contractor generally can set his or her own work hours.

8. Full-time required. An employee may be required to work or be available full-time. This indicates control by the employer. An independent contractor can work when and for whom he or she chooses.

9. Work done on premises. An employee usually works on the premises of an employer or works on a route or at a location designated by an employer.

10. Order or sequences set. An employee may be required to perform services in the order or sequence set by an employer. This shows that the employee is subject to direction and control.

11. Reports. An employee may be required to submit reports to an employer. This shows that the employer maintains a degree of control.

12. Payments. An employee is generally paid by the hour, week, or month. An independent contractor is usually paid by the job or on a straight commission.

13. Expenses. An employee's business and travel expenses are generally paid by an employer. This shows that the employee is subject to regulation and control.

14. Tools and materials. An employee is normally furnished significant tools, materials, and other equipment by an employer.

15. Investment. An independent contractor has a significant investment in the facilities he or she uses in performing services for someone else.

16. Profit or loss. An independent contractor can make a profit or suffer a loss.

17. Works for more than one person or firm. An independent contractor is generally free to provide his or her services to two or more unrelated persons or firms at the same time.

18. Offers services to general public. An independent contractor makes his or her services available to the general public.

19. Right to fire. An employee can be fired by an employer. An independent contractor cannot be fired so long as he or she produces a result that meets the specifications of the contract.

20. Right to quit. An employee can quit his or her job at any time without incurring liability. An independent contractor usually agrees to complete a specific job and is responsible for its satisfactory completion or is legally obligated to make good for failure to complete it.

Consultants' Resource Directory

Take a stroll through your local bookstore and you'll see shelf upon shelf of books designed to help people start and operate a small business. The general principles contained in these books are just as applicable to your consulting business as they are to other small businesses. In addition, there is a growing recognition of consulting as a specialized business with numerous books, magazines, and other resources now available to specifically help consultants in their business.

This directory is the result of background research accomplished by the author while writing this book. It highlights resources that focus specifically on the needs of consultants.

If readers are aware of additional resources that would be helpful to other consultants, they are welcome to contact the author directly.

Judy Gedge
18 North Main Street
West Hartford, CT 06107
jgedge@ntplx.net *email*

Associations

Just about every consulting field has an association specific to that consulting field. These associations can provide information about starting and operating a consulting business. They also provide valuable member benefits including access to liability insurance programs specific to that consulting field.

An excellent resource for finding an association in your consulting field is the *Encyclopedia of Associations*, published every year by Gale Research. You can probably find this multivolume set in the reference section of your local public library. A representative sampling of consultants' associations contained in the *Encyclopedia* is listed below. There are also several associations which cater more generally to consultants which are also listed below.

General Consultants' Associations

The American Consultants League
The Consultants Institute
30466 Prince William Street
Princess Anne, MD 21853
(410) 651-4869

This organization provides assistance to consultants in establishing and managing the business component of their consulting business. It also sells books exclusively for consultants through its publishing division, The Consultant's Library. The organization also publishes a newsletter for consultants, *Consulting Intelligence.*

Association of Part-Time Professionals
7700 Leesburg Pike, No. 216
Falls Church, VA 22043
(703) 734-7975
Internet: http://mbinet.mindbank.com/aptp

This association caters to part-time professionals including job-sharers, free-lancers, and consultants. It publishes a newsletter, *Working Options.*

Consultants National Resource Center

P.O. Box 430
Clear Springs, MD 21722
(301) 791-9332
(800) 290-3196

This organization provides general marketing and strategic planning services to consultants as well as providing services to business coaches.

Consulting Resource Center

1316 North Dallas Avenue, Suite 70
Lancaster, TX 75146
(972) 227-5326
Internet: http://www.bizhowto.com

This organization produces and distributes training materials for consultants of all disciplines. It also publishes a monthly newsletter, *Consulting Opportunities Journal*, for small consulting practices of all disciplines with special emphasis on marketing.

International Society of Speakers, Authors, and Consultants

P.O. Box 6432
Kingwood, TX 77325-6432
(800) 677-3253

This organization provides assistance to consultants in building and marketing their practices. It also publishes a newsletter, *The Professional Advisor*.

National Association for the Self-Employed

2121 Precinct Line Road
Hurst, TX 76054
(800) 232-6273
Internet: http://www.nase.org

This association broadly represents people who are self-employed. It also publishes a newsletter, *Self-Employed America*.

Associations for Specific Consulting Fields

American Association of Legal Nurse Consultants
4700 West Lake Avenue
Glenview, IL 60025
(847) 375-4713
Internet: http://www.aalnc.org

American Association of Nutritional Consultants
880 Canarios Court, Suite 210
Chula Vista, CA 91910
(888) 828-2262

American Consulting Engineers Council
1015 15th Street NW
Washington, DC 20005
(202) 347-7474
Internet: http://www.acec.org

Association of Bridal Consultants
200 Chestnutland Road
New Milford, CT 06776
(860) 355-0464

Association of Consulting Chemists and Chemical Engineers
40 West 45th Street
New York, NY 10036
(212) 983-3160

Franchise Consultants International Association
5147 South Angela Road
Memphis, TN 38117
(901) 682-2951

Independent Computer Consultants Association
11131 South Towne Square, Suite F
St. Louis, MO 63123
(800) 774-4222
Internet: http://www.icca.org

Independent Educational Consultants Association

4085 Chain Bridge Road, Suite 401
Fairfax, VA 22030
(703) 591-4850
Internet: http://www.educationalconsulting.org

Institute of Management Consultants

521 Fifth Avenue, 35th Floor
New York, NY 10175
(212) 697-8262
Internet: http://www.mcusa.org

International Association of Registered Financial Consultants

P.O. Box 504
Chesterfield, MO 63006
(314) 530-7855
Internet: http://www.iarfc.org

Investment Management Consultants Association

9101 East Kenyon Avenue, Suite 3000
Denver, CO 80237
(303) 770-3377
Internet: http://www.mca.org

National Association of Business Consultants

12121 Little Road, Suite 332
Hudson, FL 34667
(800) 390-8024
Internet: http://www.nabc-inc.com

National Bureau of Professional Management Consultants

c/o Vito A. Tanzi
2728 Fifth Avenue
San Diego, CA 92103
(619) 297-2207

Associations for Specific Consulting Fields (continued)

National Society of Environmental Consultants
P.O. Box 12528
San Antonio, TX 78212
(210) 271-0781

Qualitative Research Consultants Association
P.O. Box 7576
Arlington, VA 22207
(888) 674-7722
Internet: http://www.qrca.org

Consultant Newsletters

Most associations publish a newsletter for their membership. If you have found an association of consultants in your specific consulting field, the association's newsletter can be a good source of information. In addition, the newsletters listed below are addressed to consultants in general, rather than to specific consulting fields.

Consultants' News
Publisher: Kennedy Publications
Templeton Road
Fitzwilliam, NH 03447

(This publisher also has a mail order catalog with books about consulting called the *Consultants Bookstore*.)

Consulting Intelligence
Publisher: American Consultants League
30466 Prince William Street
Princess Anne, MD 21853

Consulting Opportunities Journal
Publisher: New Ventures Publishing Group

1316 North Dallas Avenue, Suite 70
Lancaster, TX 75146

(This publisher also has a catalog of training materials for consultants of all disciplines.)

The Professional Advisor
Publisher: International Society of Speakers, Authors, and Consultants

P.O. Box 6432
Kingwood, TX 77325

Magazines

The traditional magazines geared to small businesses, such as *Inc.* and *Entrepreneur*, contain information about small business that can be applied to your consulting business. In addition, there are several magazines focused on home-based businesses and specifically on consultants. Browse through your local bookstore and you'll see how many magazines there are for small business owners. The magazines listed below may prove helpful in your consulting business.

Entrepreneur's Home Office
c/o Entrepreneur

P.O. Box 53874
Boulder, CO 80323

Income Opportunities
c/o Income Opportunities

P.O. Box 55207
Boulder, CO 80323

Self-Employed Professional
c/o Business Media Group LLC

462 Boston Street
Topsfield, MA 01983

Magazines (continued)

Small Business Opportunities
c/o Harris Publications, Inc.
1115 Broadway
New York, NY 10010

Success
c/o Success Magazine
P.O. Box 3036
Harlan, IA 51593

The Consultant's Craft
c/o Summit Consulting Group
P.O. Box 1009
East Greenwich, RI 02818

Working At Home
c/o Success Magazine
P.O. Box 5484
Harlan, IA 51593

The Small Business Administration

The Small Business Administration (SBA) has offices throughout the country. The SBA provides a wide range of resources to assist current and prospective small businesses. Contact your local SBA office to find out about the resources available through the SBA, or for more information call the SBA answer desk.

Small Business Administration Answer Desk
(800) 827-5722

Some of the services provided by the SBA are:

- Publications. *The Resource Directory for Small Business Management* details the SBA publications designed to assist in the startup and operation of small businesses. Subject matter includes marketing strategies, financial management, recordkeeping, financing, and effective business plan preparation.

- Seminars and workshops. Your local SBA office can provide you with a calendar of seminars and workshops that it sponsors for small business owners. Topics covered in these programs generally include preparation of an effective business plan, financial management and recordkeeping, marketing, and legal requirements for small businesses.

- Business Information Centers (BIC). A number of SBA offices have recently opened BICs to help their small business constituency. These centers provide the latest in high-tech hardware, software, and telecommunications for small businesses. Contact your local SBA office to find your nearest BIC.

- Service Corps of Retired Executives (SCORE). SCORE volunteers are former business executives who provide free management and technical expertise for small businesses.

- Small Business Development Centers (SBDC). The SBDCs offer a wide range of business information and guidance in the form of workshops and individual counseling for start-up and existing businesses. Contact your SBA office to find the nearest SBDC office.

- SBA financing. SBA provides a wide range of SBA-guaranteed financing including a low documentation program (LowDoc) for loans up to $100,000. The LowDoc application is a one-page form, and the SBA provides a quick response to these loan requests of usually within two days.

Internal Revenue Service

The IRS has numerous publications with information about the federal tax laws that apply to businesses. These include:

- Publication 334, *Tax Guide for Small Business*;
- Publication 583, *Starting a Business and Keeping Records*;

- Publication 1779, *Employee Independent Contractor Brochure*;
- Publication 1518, *Tax Tips, A Calendar for Small Businesses*; and
- Publication 454, *Your Business Tax Kit,* which contains various business tax forms and publications to help in preparing your business tax returns.

You can call the IRS for more information or to order IRS publications.

Internal Revenue Service
(800) 829-3676

Additional Resources

You can get loads of helpful information at your local public library. Reference materials can help you locate associations in your field as well as useful information to start or grow your consulting business. In addition, check with your local community colleges which often teach courses in business management and the like. Your state probably has one or more economic development agencies that can provide you information about the legal requirements of running a small business in your state.

Legal Terminology

Articles of organization

The organizing document under which a limited liability company is formed in accordance with the laws of a particular state.

Breach of contract

The failure of a party to perform its obligations in accordance with the terms of the contract.

Bylaws

The rules and regulations under which a corporation is governed. The bylaws address such issues as quorum and voting requirements for shareholders, election of directors, and duties of officers of the corporation.

C corporation

A corporation, formed under the laws of a particular state, which is taxable under Subchapter C of the Internal Revenue Code.

Certificate of incorporation

The organizing document under which a corporation is formed in accordance with the laws of a particular state.

Close corporation

A corporation, formed under the corporation law of some states, which consists of a limited number of shareholders that is operated less formally than a traditional corporation.

Common law

The system of law which originated in England and was later adopted in the United States which is based on case law as opposed to statutory law.

Company

A generic term applied to any business venture. A business using the word company in its name can, for instance, refer to a corporation, a partnership, or even a sole proprietor.

Compensatory damages

Money damages which are recoverable for a breach of contract and which are intended to provide to the injured party the benefit of the bargain as contracted for.

Consequential damages

Damages suffered from a breach of contract which are not the direct result of the breach but result from a consequence of the breach.

Consideration

Something of value given in return for performance or an agreement to perform under a contract. Consideration is generally a prerequisite to the enforcement of a contract.

Contract

An agreement between two or more persons which creates an obligation to perform or refrain from performing particular actions.

Copyright

The protection granted by law to the creator of original works fixed in a tangible medium, including such works as books, drawings, computer software, graphics, pictures, and audio and video tapes.

Corporation

An association formed under the laws of a particular state which has a legal existence separate and apart from the principals of the organization. The principals of a corporation generally do not incur personal liability for the obligations of the corporation.

dba

Abbreviation of 'doing business as' which identifies the business name under which a business is operated; also referred to as a tradename.

Employee

A person retained to provide services for an employer and over whom the employer has the right to control in detail the manner in which the services are provided. The classification of a worker as an employee instead of as an independent contractor can have significant legal and tax consequences for the employer.

General partnership

An association of two or more persons engaged in business in which the individuals share in the profits and losses of the business venture. Also referred to as a partnership. See also joint venture.

Guarantee

An assurance that a product or service will satisfy specified requirements, similar to a warranty.

Independent contractor

A person retained to provide services who retains control of the manner of producing the desired results. The classification of a worker as an employee instead of as an independent contractor can have significant legal and tax consequences for the employer.

Joint venture

An association of two or more persons engaging in a specific business in which the individuals share in the profits and losses of the business venture. A joint venture is similar to a general partnership but denotes an enterprise of limited scope.

Limited liability company

An association formed under the laws of a particular state which has a legal existence separate and apart from the principals of the organization. The principals of a limited liability company generally do not incur personal liability for the obligations of the company.

Limited liability partnership

An association formed under the laws of a particular state under which the personal liability of the partners is limited in accordance with the governing state statute.

Limited partnership

An association of two or more persons formed under the laws of a particular state to engage in business in which at least one partner, the general partner, is personally liable for the obligations of the partnership and manages the business affairs of the partnership. The other partners, the limited partners, do not participate in the management of the partnership.

Manager

The person who has the authority to take actions as the agent of a limited liability company in accordance with the provisions of its operating agreement. A limited liability company can be manager-operated or member-operated.

Operating agreement

The contract entered into by the members of a limited liability company setting forth the operating rules for the company, such as whether the company will be operated by a manager or by the members. It generally addresses the percentage ownership interests of each member, the capital contributions or loans to be made to the company by the members, and voting rights of members.

P.C. (professional corporation)

A corporation formed under the laws of a particular state for the purpose of engaging in specific licensed occupations, such as medicine, law, or accounting.

Piercing the corporate veil

The action taken by courts in disregarding the protection accorded corporate or limited liability entities and instead imposing personal liability on the principals of the entity when fraud or other factors are involved.

S corporation

A corporation, formed under the laws of a particular state, which is taxed under Subchapter S of the Internal Revenue Code. An S corporation is treated like a partnership for federal tax purposes.

Sole Proprietorship

A business owned and operated by one person. There is no legal distinction between the business and its owner, therefore, the owner has unlimited personal liability for the obligations of the business.

Statute of Frauds

A statute derived from a 16th century English statute which requires certain contracts to be in writing to be enforceable.

Subcontractor

A person who enters into a contract with a prime contractor to perform a portion of the services which the prime contractor has contracted to perform for a third party.

Index

A

accountant, see: business accountant

agreements
    consulting 49–58, 65–70
    subcontractor 56–57, 71–75

The American Consultants League 82

associations for consultants
    general 82–83
    specific fields 84–86

attorney, see: lawyers

B

breach of contract 7–8, 27, 35–36, 56

business accountant 19, 23

C

C corporation 18–20
    shareholders 16–17
    structure 16–18, 20, 22, 62–63
    tax treatment 18

close corporation (closely held) 18, 30

common law 26

confidentiality agreement 54, 68

consultant associations 82–86

consultant newsletters 86
    Consultants' News 86
    Consulting Intelligence 82, 86
    Consulting Opportunities Journal 83, 87
    The Professional Advisor 83, 87

P

partnership liability 10–12

payroll taxes 42–44, 47

    contractor responsibility 29

    employer 42–43

    trust fund taxes 29

personal guarantees 7, 25–26, 30

piercing the corporate veil 26, 30–31

potential liability 1–7, 9–11, 13–14, 25–26

professional corporation, see: limited liability partnership

R

resources, for consultants 81–90

S

S corporation 15, 20–21

    structure 20

    tax treatment 20–21

sales tax 28, 69

self-employment tax 43

shareholder 17, 19–21

sole proprietor 1–2, 8–9, 15, 28

Statute of Frauds 35

strategic alliance 4–5, 10, 14

    potential liability 4–6, 10

subcontractor agreements 56–57, 71–75

T

taxes 19–21, 29, 42–44, 47, 68, 74, 77

    employer 29, 42–43, 47, 77

    independent contractor 43, 77

    sales tax 28

    trust fund 29

W

workers compensation 44–45

Z

zoning laws 28–29

From The Leading Publisher of Small Business Information
Books that save you time and money.

Managers and business owners will learn exactly where to draw the line on sexual harassment. How to draw the line firmly, so that employees understand and respect it. Clearly spells out the procedures that are most effective if a lawsuit is lodged and gives tips on enlisting a good attorney.

Draw The Line   **Pages: 172**
Paperback: $17.95   ISBN: 1-55571-370-X

This useful guide discusses techniques for developing a solid foundation on which to build a successful business. Includes many real-world pointers that any business can implement into its day-to-day operations. Contains 30 checklists, evaluations, figures, and charts that will give you the power to drive your business' profits in the right direction.

Profit Power   **Pages: 272**
Paperback: $19.95   ISBN: 1-55571-374-2

Saves costly consultant or staff hours in creating company personnel policies. Provides over 70 model policies on topics such as employee safety, leave of absence, flex time, smoking, substance abuse, sexual harassment, performance improvement, and grievance procedures. For each subject, practical and legal ramifications are explained and a choice of alternate policies is presented.

Company Policy & Personnel Workbook   **Pages: 350**
Paperback: $29.95   ISBN: 1-55571-365-3
Binder: $49.95   ISBN: 1-55571-364-5

Surviving Success presents a program for those who wish to lead their companies from promising startup to industry dominance. Meet the challenges of business growth and transition with new insights. Learn from success stories. Be prepared to take proactive steps into your company's next growth transition.

Surviving Success   **Pages: 230**
Paperback: $19.95   ISBN: 1-55571-446-3

From The Leading Publisher of Small Business Information

Books that save you time and money.

If you can't remember the last time you found yourself smiling at work, it's time to read *Joysticks, Blinking Lights, and Thrills*. A refreshing approach to running your business or department within a business. Shows where, how, and why most small business problems could occur and what can be done to resolve them. Sherlock brings humorous examples from his own business experiences to identify over 45 specific problem areas in business and their easy-to-implement solutions.

Joysticks, Blinking Lights, & Thrills　　　　　**Pages: 275**
Paperback: $18.95　　　**ISBN: 1-55571-401-3**

This innovative book provides managers with an entirely new way of looking at information that can save time, money, headaches, and maybe even their jobs or companies. It provides cutting-edge principles and concepts that will help people work far more effectively and easily with all sorts of data.

Information Breakthrough　　　　　**Pages: 250**
Paperback: $22.95　　　**ISBN: 1-55571-413-7**

Focuses on developing the art of working with people to maximize the productivity and satisfaction of both manager and employees. Discussions, exercises, and self-tests boost skill in communicating, delegating, motivating, developing teams, goal-setting, adapting to change, and coping with stress.

Managing People　　　　　**Pages: 260**
Paperback: $21.95　　　**ISBN: 1-55571-380-7**

Author Luigi Salvaneschi clearly shows how studying eight specific liberal arts principles can help nurture your own leadership skills within — and make you an asset for the business world of the 21st century. Each chapter leads you through his new concept in management thinking and tells how it applies to both the business world and your own personal life. Includes exercises to explore at home, work, and while traveling.

Renaissance 2000　　　　　**Pages: 345**
Paperback: $22.95　　　**ISBN: 1-55571-412-9**

The Oasis Press® Order Form

LRMC06/98

Call, Mail, Email, or Fax Your Order to: PSI Research, P.O. Box 3727, Central Point, OR 97502
Email: sales@psi-research.com   Website: http://www.psi-research.com
Order Phone USA & Canada: +1 800 228-2275   Inquiries & International Orders: +1 541 479-9464 Fax: +1 541 476-1479

TITLE	✔ BINDER	✔ PAPERBACK	QUANTITY	COST
Advertising Without An Agency		❑ $19.95		
Bottom Line Basics	❑ $39.95	❑ $19.95		
BusinessBasics: A Microbusiness Startup Guide		❑ $17.95		
The Business Environmental Handbook	❑ $39.95	❑ $19.95		
Business Owner's Guide to Accounting & Bookkeeping		❑ $19.95		
Buyer's Guide to Business Insurance	❑ $39.95	❑ $19.95		
California Corporation Formation Package	❑ $39.95	❑ $29.95		
Collection Techniques for a Small Business	❑ $39.95	❑ $19.95		
A Company Policy and Personnel Workbook	❑ $49.95	❑ $29.95		
Company Relocation Handbook	❑ $39.95	❑ $19.95		
CompControl: The Secrets of Reducing Worker's Compensation Costs	❑ $39.95	❑ $19.95		
Complete Book of Business Forms		❑ $19.95		
Connecting Online: Creating a Successful Image on the Internet		❑ $21.95		
Customer Engineering: Cutting Edge Selling Strategies	❑ $39.95	❑ $19.95		
Develop & Market Your Creative Ideas		❑ $15.95		
Developing International Markets		❑ $19.95		
Doing Business in Russia		❑ $19.95		
Draw The Line: A Sexual Harassment Free Workplace		❑ $17.95		
Entrepreneurial Decisionmaking		❑ $19.95		
The Essential Corporation Handbook		❑ $21.95		
the Essential Limited Liability Company Handbook	❑ $39.95	❑ $21.95		
Export Now: A Guide for Small Business	❑ $39.95	❑ $24.95		
Financial Decisionmaking: A Guide for the Non-Accountant		❑ $19.95		
Financial Management Techniques for Small Business	❑ $39.95	❑ $19.95		
Financing Your Small Business		❑ $19.95		
Franchise Bible: How to Buy a Franchise or Franchise Your Own Business	❑ $39.95	❑ $24.95		
Friendship Marketing: Growing Your Business by Cultivating Strategic Relationships		❑ $18.95		
Funding High-Tech Ventures		❑ $21.95		
Home Business Made Easy		❑ $19.95		
Information Breakthrough		❑ $22.95		
The Insider's Guide to Small Business Loans	❑ $29.95	❑ $19.95		
InstaCorp – Incorporate In Any State (Book & Software)		❑ $29.95		
Joysticks, Blinking Lights and Thrills		❑ $18.95		
Keeping Score: An Inside Look at Sports Marketing		❑ $18.95		
Know Your Market: How to Do Low-Cost Market Research	❑ $39.95	❑ $19.95		
The Leader's Guide		❑ $19.95		
Legal Expense Defense: How to Control Your Business' Legal Costs and Problems	❑ $39.95	❑ $19.95		
Location, Location, Location: How to Select the Best Site for Your Business		❑ $19.95		
Mail Order Legal Guide	❑ $45.00	❑ $29.95		
Managing People: A Practical Guide		❑ $21.95		
Marketing for the New Millennium: Applying New Techniques		❑ $19.95		
Marketing Mastery: Your Seven Step Guide to Success	❑ $39.95	❑ $19.95		
The Money Connection: Where and How to Apply for Business Loans and Venture Capital	❑ $39.95	❑ $24.95		
Moonlighting: Earn a Second Income at Home		❑ $15.95		
People Investment	❑ $39.95	❑ $19.95		
Power Marketing for Small Business	❑ $39.95	❑ $19.95		
Profit Power: 101 Pointers to Give Your Business a Competitive Edge		❑ $19.95		
Proposal Development: How to Respond and Win the Bid	❑ $39.95	❑ $21.95		
Raising Capital		❑ $19.95		
Renaissance 2000: Liberal Arts Essentials for Tomorrow's Leaders		❑ $22.95		
Retail in Detail: How to Start and Manage a Small Retail Business		❑ $15.95		
Secrets to High Ticket Selling		❑ $19.95		
Secrets to Buying and Selling a Business		❑ $24.95		
Secure Your Future: Financial Planning at Any Age	❑ $39.95	❑ $19.95		
The Small Business Insider's Guide to Bankers		❑ $18.95		
SmartStart Your (State) Business... series		❑ $19.95		
PLEASE SPECIFY WHICH STATE(S) YOU WANT:				
Smile Training Isn't Enough: The Three Secrets to Excellent Customer Service		❑ $19.95		
Start Your Business (Available as a book and disk package)		❑ $ 9.95 (without disk)		

BOOK SUB-TOTAL (Additional titles on other side)

TITLE	✔ BINDER	✔ PAPERBACK	QUANTITY	COST
Starting and Operating a Business in...series *Includes FEDERAL section PLUS ONE STATE section*	☐ $34.95	☐ $27.95		
PLEASE SPECIFY WHICH STATE(S) YOU WANT:				
STATE SECTION ONLY (BINDER NOT INCLUDED) SPECIFY STATE(S):	☐ $8.95			
FEDERAL SECTION ONLY (BINDER NOT INCLUDED)	☐ $12.95			
U.S. EDITION (FEDERAL SECTION – 50 STATES AND WASHINGTON DC IN 11-BINDER SET)	☐ $295.95			
Successful Business Plan: Secrets & Strategies	☐ $49.95	☐ $27.95		
Successful Network Marketing for The 21st Century		☐ $15.95		
Surviving Success		☐ $19.95		
TargetSmart! Database Marketing for the Small Business		☐ $19.95		
Top Tax Saving Ideas for Today's Small Business		☐ $16.95		
Twenty-One Sales in a Sale: What Sales Are You Missing?		☐ $19.95		
Which Business? Help in Selecting Your New Venture		☐ $18.95		
Write Your Own Business Contracts	☐ $39.95	☐ $24.95		
BOOK SUB-TOTAL (Be sure to figure your amount from the previous side)				

OASIS SOFTWARE Please specify which computer operating system you use (DOS, MacOS, or Windows)

TITLE	✔ Windows	✔ MacOS	Price	QUANTITY	COST
California Corporation Formation Package ASCII Software	☐	☐	$ 39.95		
Company Policy & Personnel Software Text Files	☐	☐	$ 49.95		
Financial Management Techniques (Full Standalone)	☐		$ 99.95		
Financial Templates	☐	☐	$ 69.95		
The Insurance Assistant Software (Full Standalone)	☐		$ 29.95		
Start Your Business (Software for Windows™)	☐		$ 19.95		
Successful Business Plan (Software for Windows™)	☐		$ 99.95		
Successful Business Plan Templates	☐		$ 69.95		
The Survey Genie - Customer Edition (Full Standalone)	☐ $199.95 (WIN)	☐ $149.95 (DOS)			
The Survey Genie - Employee Edition (Full Standalone)	☐ $199.95 (WIN)	☐ $149.95 (DOS)			
SOFTWARE SUB-TOTAL					

BOOK & DISK PACKAGES Please specify which computer operating system you use (DOS, MacOS, or Windows)

TITLE	✔ Windows	✔ MacOS	✔ Binder	✔ Paperback	QUANTITY	COST
The Buyer's Guide to Business Insurance w/ Insurance Assistant	☐		☐ $ 59.95	☐ $ 39.95		
California Corporation Formation Binder Book & ASCII Software	☐	☐	☐ $ 69.95	☐ $ 59.95		
Company Policy & Personnel Book & Software Text Files	☐	☐	☐ $ 89.95	☐ $ 69.95		
Financial Management Techniques Book & Software	☐		☐ $129.95	☐ $ 119.95		
Start Your Business Paperback & Software (Software for Windows™)	☐			☐ $ 24.95		
Successful Business Plan Book & Software for Windows™	☐		☐ $125.95	☐ $109.95		
Successful Business Plan Book & Software Templates	☐	☐	☐ $109.95	☐ $ 89.95		
BOOK & DISK PACKAGE SUB-TOTAL						

AUDIO CASSETTES

Power Marketing Tools For Small Business			☐ $ 49.95		
The Secrets To Buying & Selling A Business			☐ $ 49.95		
AUDIO CASSETTES SUB-TOTAL					

Sold To: Please give street address

NAME:

Title:

Company:

Street Address:

City/State/Zip:

Daytime Phone: Email:

Your Grand Total

SUB-TOTALS (from other side)	$	
SUB-TOTALS (from this side)	$	
SHIPPING (see chart below)	$	
TOTAL ORDER	$	

Ship To: If different than above, please give alternate street address

NAME:

Title:

Company:

Street Address:

City/State/Zip:

Daytime Phone:

If your purchase is:	Shipping costs within the USA:
$0 - $25	$5.00
$25.01 - $50	$6.00
$50.01 - $100	$7.00
$100.01 - $175	$9.00
$175.01 - $250	$13.00
$250.01 - $500	$18.00
$500.01+	4% of total merchandise

06/98

Payment Information: Rush service is available, call for details.
International and Canadian Orders: Please call for quote on shipping.

☐ CHECK Enclosed payable to PSI Research   Charge: ☐ VISA   ☐ MASTERCARD   ☐ AMEX   ☐ DISCOVER

Card Number: Expires:

Signature: Name On Card: